The Cows of Hobson's Pond
Mostly True Stories of Growing Up Kansas

Other books by Rick McNary

Fiction
Voices on the Prairie

Non-fiction
Hunger Bites: Bite Size Stories of Inspiration

Rick McNary
521 Whispering Meadows
Potwin, KS 67123

www.rickmcnary.me
rick@whisperingmeadows.com
316-734-6845

The Cows of Hobson's Pond
Mostly True Stories of Growing Up Kansas

Rick McNary

Published by
Whispering Meadows Press
A Division of

Whispering Meadows
COMPANY
capturing the heart of your story

Copyright

Dedication

I dedicate this book to my sister, Carmen Miller. I was thirty-years-old before I realized she was my sister and not my Mom. The reason is her children are all my age so they were more like siblings and Carmen more like a mother. You will also discover in these stories her children are the reason for any and all mischief in which I found myself in as a child.

In my early thirties, Carmen made the transition from being a Mom to that of a sister then that of my best friend.

Before each one of these stories saw the light of day, I would call Carmen and read them to her. At times, we both laughed so much we had to hang up the phone and call each other back when we settled down.

Aside from being my confidant, my counselor and my friend, Carmen is my hero.

Somewhere, some cow's therapist knows everything there is to know about Rick McNary.

Prologue

Writing Until I Make Myself Laugh

When I started writing my novel, ***Voices on the Prairie,*** I took the advice of E.L. Doctorow who said that *writing was like driving at night; you can only see as far as the headlights.*

After writing *The Cows of Hobson's Pond*, I would add: *you also need to look in the rearview mirror ever once in a while to see what you ran over in the road.*

I started off the humor series to chronicle mostly true stories of my youth. I now look back at what I ran over in the road and realize that *The Cows of Hobson's Pond* play a significant role during my formative years. My imagination took flight about the same time our naked little bodies streaked across a Kansas pasture. Some people blame their parents for everything that's wrong in their life. Not me, I blame the Cows of Hobson's Pond.

As a writer, this series taught me a lot about writing that I didn't know. For example, I did not know I could make myself laugh while writing. In the first story of us three little boys streaking home naked from Hobson's Pond, I busted out laughing at six o'clock in the morning as I wrote. My wife checked on me to see if I was okay and I said I'd told myself a joke I'd never heard before. She walked off muttering something about *who in their right mind laughs at his own writings at six o'clock in the morning?*

Making myself laugh has become my standard for each of these stories. I write, re-write, and re-write again until I make myself laugh. Hopefully, you laugh, too, but by the time you've read it, I've already had a good chuckle or two. I'm kind of simple that way; I can entertain myself.

Every writer writes for both a *known* audience and an *unknown* audience. The *known* audience for these stories of my youth is made up of eight people, seven of whom can't read or write yet. Those seven are my grandkids; someday they'll read this and it will make complete sense why they think cows can talk. The eighth is my older sister, Carmen, whose children are a part of these stories. Her children are also to blame with what's wrong with the other parts of me that the cows didn't tarnish. I learned early the American way: accept no responsibility and always play the victim.

The *unknown* audience is people I've never met like the lady from Australia who lived for a period of time in Kansas with her children. She wrote to tell me how homesick the stories made her for Kansas.

The title is not a misprint. The phrase, Growing Up Kansas, started by accident, but I kept it as a souvenir. A person once asked me what my childhood was like and I meant to say, *I grew up **in** Kansas.* Instead, I said, *I grew up Kansas.* The person said explained a lot about me and I agree; Kansas isn't so much a place as it is a state of mind.

Each time I write a story, I call Carmen on the phone to read it to her. Writing a humorous story is very different than telling a joke. With a joke, you get to hear people laugh. With a story of humor, you just hope someone writes back to you and tells you it was funny.

My sister makes for a great audience because she knows the players in the story and, as a person, has more fun tickets than most people I know; she laughs easily and sweetly.

She laughs when I read the stories; she cries when I read the stories; she reminds me of things I had forgotten; and she apologizes for letting Jeff and Colleen torment me so much.

And always, and I mean every bloody time, she says this: *those poor cows.* She feels sorry for The Cows of Hobson's Pond and the manner in which I portray them. However, I argue I'm actually being much nicer to them than they were to me.

A friend once told me I'm an anthropomorphic writer. I told him to wait right where he stood while I looked that word up 'cause I might have to punch him for insulting me. It turns out he wasn't questioning my heritage after all; he was saying that I give human-like qualities to non-human beings like the Cows of Hobson's Pond. I won that argument when I reminded him that the Chik-fil-A cows could read and write. My logic was flawless.

Each book has a dedication section and I would be remiss not to dedicate this book to The Cows of Hobson's Pond. I suppose I'll list Gertrude, May Belle, Claudine, Nettie, and Frances, since they were my favorites. But I sure hope I don't hurt the feelings of the rest of them like Flo, Hazel, Henrietta, and Eudene.

I make it a point not to offend any cows these days. I'm just getting too old to be chased across any more pastures.

P.S. Would you be kind enough to go to Amazon some time and write a sentence or two review about this book? Amazon pays attention to the number of reviews a book receives and will actually help market it rather just let it set on a digital bookshelf. Admittedly, I'd love a 5-star review, but would prefer your honesty.

Go to: www.amazon.com

Then look for, *The Cows of Hobson's Pond.*

Once you find it, you will see a place you can submit a review.

You can find my other books there, too.

Voices on the Prairie

Hunger Bites: Bite Size Stories of Inspiration

The Day We Invented Streaking

F olks who that say that driving thru Kansas is boring have never seen three little boys streaking thru the pasture with pond mud forming makeshift loincloths. That happened at least once I'll admit to.

The drafty old two-story farmhouse in rural Kansas that I grew up in originally sat far enough from the busy two-lane Highway 54 to be safe. However, the state decided to move the highway close enough to our house that we sometimes had to open the front door to let cars pass each other.

Down the highway to the east of the house about ½ of a mile was Hobson's Pond. It was glorious place of our youth that, at the time, seemed as vast, deep and mysterious as the Atlantic Ocean teeming with aquatic animals and humpback whales. Instead, our pond had finger-length bullhead catfish that swam up your shorts and impaled you with poison-tipped barbs and cantankerous cows that cooled their udders in the water like they thought it was a spa.

Usually, we ran the cows out of the pond only to turn around and have to outrun the cows. Cows are not only fast; they are sarcastic. Cows are the little old ladies of the animal kingdom who love to comment on about how the youth of today are going to hell-in-a-hand basket.

"Hey, Maude!" Gertrude the cow shouted as we raced across the prairie dodging their strategically placed cow pies, "Look at this skinny one run. I bet I can catch him this time before he darts under the barbwire fence."

Since I was the baby of the family with siblings old enough to have children my age, my nieces and nephews were my peers. Each summer, three of them would descend upon me from New York. Sometimes, two others appeared randomly and turned my bored-out-of-my-mind existence on the lonesome prairie into four weeks of sermons on morals, groundings, and spankings, sometimes all the above.

There were an equal number of girls and boys all within a four-year age range so it was easy to form alliances against the enemy: boys against girls. Since we were the boys, it was assumed any mischief originated in our devious little minds. When shenanigans erupted, the boys were lined up in front of the firing squad first. No questions; no jury of our peers; just the judge handing out verdicts without due process.

We didn't have such things at swimming suits, just cut off jeans. If we didn't have those, we were not a bit bashful about skinny-dipping. The three of us boys managed to escape the scorn of cows and, since we didn't own such a thing as a swimming suit, decided to frolic in Hobson's Pond in our birthday suit. The cows were so sarcastic we dared not let them see us in our birthday suits.

We froze when we saw the girls sneaking through the grass headed to our clothes. We dared not emerge from the water lest we traumatize both the girls and ourselves, so we just sat there like three fat toads on a log watching them steal our clothes. Above the giggling of the girls, we heard the cows snickering in the background.

The girls took off towards home with our clothes in hand. Even our shoes.

The line from Hobson's Pond to our house ran parallel to Highway 54, the busiest stretch of blacktop in Kansas. Furthermore, it was only about fifty feet away so we were assured an audience of passersby. There were no fig leave to protect our shame and we knew better than to wrap ourselves in poison ivy so we used the next best thing; pond mud.

The bottom of a Kansas pond has the consistency of warm Jell-O, the toxicity of a nuclear reactor, and the adhesive qualities of Teflon. It is not the optimal clothing to hide one's form. I keep expecting to see Miley Cyrus wearing it on the red carpet.

Furthermore, since we hadn't quite matured yet, our bodies were mainly hairless, so there was absolutely nothing for the mud to adhere to. But we grabbed some up, packed ourselves with it, and took off on a dead run.

We lost most of it in the first fifteen feet of our dash home. By that time, horns were honking, vacationers were stopping to take pictures, and the cows laughed so hard their milk turned into cottage cheese.

Let it be noted that there are few things more frightening than crawling through a barbwire fence while naked.

We made it home only to find out that we, not the girls, were in trouble. Apparently the powers-that-be ruling the farmhouse - namely the Matriarchs of the clan - determined that the boys were responsible for any and all crimes against humanity. We were lined up, tied to a stake, and the fires of righteous indignation lit at our feet.

However, vengeance is the Lord's and the next story will be how we were vindicated, and felt pretty darn smug about it. Naturally, we got in trouble over that, too, but it was worth it.

I often wonder if, at some dining room table at Thanksgiving somewhere in the U.S., some family says, "Hey, remember that time we were driving across Kansas and those three little boys were streaking through the pasture!" They laugh, dig out the photos they took of us, then say to each other, "Well, whoever says Kansas is boring has never seen a cow laughing so hard it blows milk out its nose."

Come to Kansas. We'll wow ya.

The Real Cold War in Kansas

All good men have their enemies; Reagan had Solzhenitsyn; Kennedy had Castro; Rocky Balboa had Apollo Creed; I had Colleen Miller. She was my niece, nemesis and bane of my prepubescent existence. I was thirty-years-old before I could hear her name without curling up in a fetal position.

During my youth, there was The Cold War and The Real Cold War. On the macrocosm, The Cold War was, of course, between the U.S. and the Soviet Union. However, on the microcosm, The Real Cold War was between my niece, Colleen Miller, and me. Fifty weeks out of the year, half a continent separated us so all was quiet on the western and eastern fronts; she lived in New York and I in Kansas. Over fourteen hundred miles of distance kept our missiles in their underground silos as our fellow soldiers enjoyed peacetime recreation. We couldn't have hurt each other if we tried.

5

However, two weeks out of a year, we came within firing range when she came on vacation with her family to Kansas. War plans collecting dust and weapons with rusted firing pins were hauled out of the closet, dusted off, oiled, and bayonets sharpened. Lines were drawn in the sand, allies were bribed, threatened, or shamed into allegiance, and new uniforms issued.

The war should have been relatively fair because there were an equal number of genders on each side; three girls and three boys. What the boys didn't understand until well into manhood was that the number of females engaged in combat was actually six instead of three because of the matriarchs of the family – also known as the Three Generals - who always took the sides of the girls. Always. Really, I mean always. Not once do I recall the boys ever having the support of the Three Generals.

Most of our existence was armed neutrality. A skirmish would erupt on the flanks, we would have to apologize for our existence to the girls and the entire female species, and then we'd play in the vicinity of each other keeping a watchful eye on any subversive activity. Each side would send the occasional drone for reconnaissance, but we came to accept the fact that the girls were far better at spying than the boys. They were also far more secretive about their plans. One of the boys - whose name I won't mention - folded like a two-dollar suitcase under interrogation by the females. He not only gave up vital battle plans and ciphers to our well-crafted codes, he fought on their side occasionally. Oh, the shame.

Both sides had their field generals; we had Jeff and the girls had Colleen. Jeff and Colleen happened to be brother and sister so they were well aware of each other's war strategies. Colleen and her soldiers also had the Three Generals providing logistical support, counter intelligence and legal counsel. We never had a chance, but that didn't keep us from relishing small victories. Like the Native Americans who once roamed our prairie and retold stories of heroism around the campfires, to this day when we get together we relive those glory days when, on occasion, we happened to get lucky and win a temporary skirmish.

The Cows of Hobson's Pond

After *The Day We Invented Streaking* - when the girls snuck up and stole our clothes while we were skinny dipping - we all decided to go swimming in Hobson's Pond.

My Dad, who was not the best carpenter in the world, but understood the importance of a good swimming hole, erected a wooden dock on the edge of the pond. As was in line with Dad's limited carpentry skills, the posts rotted out so the dock laid half in and half out of the water. Over the course of time, moss covered the dock and, when wet, made a short, but slippery slide.

The boys wore cutoffs and wallowed around in the pond reminiscent of baby buffalo. The girls wore bathing suits which, it turns out, provide minimal protection to the Gluteus Maximus as compared to a good pair of cutoff jean-shorts.

When Colleen screamed at volume 5 on a scale from 1-10, her voice could shatter fine crystal and the Three Generals would come rushing to execute judgment. She did this often. But this fateful day as us boys were dunking each other in the middle of the pond, Colleen let out a scream so loud that even the cows started stampeding. Usually, the cows were on the side of the girls and normally would have joined in on the chorus with her, but after dodging lighting strikes on the prairie in thunderstorms, they were a bit skittish with loud noises.

We quickly discovered that in her slide down the dock, a big, nasty splinter gouged her right in the butt-cheek then broke off. Those splinters were nasty because they were so rotten that when you grabbed them with tweezers, they crumbled.

She ran screaming through the pasture like a newly branded calf with us in hot pursuit. Why were we chasing her? To help, of course. We were gentlemen; we would help any damsel in distress even if she were our part-time enemy. Plus, we'd never seen a splinter so big in human body and the gross-out factor fascinated us.

Naturally, we got in trouble for it. When the Three Generals looked out the door towards the east and saw six little kids running through the pasture and the one in the lead bellowing like a bull moose, they always concluded it was the boys' fault. Always.

I don't recall what kind of punishment was handed out to us, but the biggest disappointment was not being allowed to dig that monstrosity out of her butt-cheek. Heck, we would have been happy just to watch. However, we took some comfort in being able to hear it all. We spent the rest of the summer replacing the storm windows she shattered with her screams.

As the Three Generals dragged us off to the Gulag for another round of imprisonment, we congratulated each other for our valiant efforts to assist the wounded. While incarcerated, we all agreed that those lingering doubts we'd been having about the existence of God would from henceforth and forevermore be removed. There was a God who avenged us innocent boys at least one time out of fifty.

A temporary armistice was signed between the warring factions to allow the wounded to heal. Weapons were laid down; spoils were divided; we sang songs of heroism around the campfire and olive branches were offered for lasting peace.

Little did we know that our skirmishes paled in comparison to the next threat to our existence: extraterrestrials in UFOs.

The Night the UFO's Came to Get Us

It's not every day that six little country kids in Kansas have UFOs show up in their backyard and scare the bejesus out of them.

During the late sixties, there was an uptick in UFO sightings across the U.S. There was also an uptick in the use of LSD. I'm not saying that the two are tied together, but the universe does have a cause-and-effect correlation.

However, we six little kids stuck in a drafty old two-story house for a few weeks each summer were LSD free. The closest we ever got to getting stoned was sniffing the old Schnapps and Jack Daniels bottles thrown in the ditch by passing tourists. We roamed the ditches along Highway 54 looking for pop bottles to cash in at the grocery store but found a disproportionate number of whiskey bottles. After three good snorts of Schnapps one day, we swore off alcohol forever.

Back to the aliens. You might think I digress, but after years of contemplation, light has illuminated my darkness with an epiphany: the UFO showed up the same day as we snorted the Schnapps. I told you there was a correlation.

Six little kids intuitively knew better than to hang inside Command Central all day when the Three Generals were lurking about. We hit the back door shortly after breakfast with packed lunches and crawled back in at dark. We did this not so much for the fresh air and adventure as self-preservation. To be near the Three Generals meant that one was quickly forced into slave labor or, as was the case for us boys, held responsible for all things wrong in the world. The girls stayed inside more than we, but they were always *the most-highly-favored-among-men-and-angel*s. Always.

I'm not saying the girls were from the devil, but we did not share the same lofty opinion of them that, say, the Three Generals or the Commander-in Chief and his Secretary of War. Ah, you haven't met these two yet?

The Commander-in-Chief was my Dad; the Secretary of War, Tom, was his son-in-law and father to half of the six miscreants. They were married to two of the Three Generals. Nepotism in the ranks always creates disorder in the chain of command, but things were what they were. One of the Three Generals didn't have a husband at the time and emptied her frustrations with the adult male species on the juvenile male species; namely, us.

The Commander-in-Chief and the Secretary of War were normally gentle giants who graced our presence with wisdom, justice and mercy. The Three Generals were like BB guns annoying you with stinging shots, but the Commander and Secretary were the Howitzers. However, they, like us boys, left the house as soon as breakfast was over for various hunter-gatherer activities.

Some days we extended our outside activities into sleeping outside, depending on the degree to which we annoyed the Generals during the day. We didn't have fancy tents or sleeping bags, but we did have The Cabin and The Shed.

The Cabin was a little shack my Dad dragged home from the oilfield. Dotted around the oilfields of Kansas beside grasshopper-looking pump-jacks were little 12'x12' buildings called doghouses. I don't know how, but Dad managed to place one along the hedgerow north of the house about 50 yards. That was as close as he would ever get to his dream of living in a cabin in the mountains. A little potbelly wood stove tucked in the corner and an old bed, chair and nightstand made it a comfy little place.

The three girls slept in there when they wanted because, well, they were *the most-highly-favored-among-men-and-angels*, so they got whatever they wanted. Always. We boys, on the other hand, got the Shed.

The Shed was a lean-to on the back of the garage. It was a 15-degree sloping roof that extended ten feet north of the garage. That's where the boys camped out; the girls got The Cabin; the boys got The Shed.

The Shed had two inherent problems:

- It had no roof because, well, it was a roof to something else.
- It had a fifteen-degree slope. I woke up one morning with legs dangling over the edge from the knees down.

Had we a tent, we would have happily spent every summer night in it. But the thought of sleeping in the open on the ground gave us the heebie-jeebies. We blamed it on the grass and chiggers, but our secret fears were being dragged off by the coyotes, poisoned by spiders, or waking up to a rattlesnake curled up between our legs.

I'll be honest; there are various interpretations of the following events depending on which of the six little kids you talk to. I maintain mine is the closest to the truth and the others are simply revisionist historians.

The Cows of Hobson's Pond

Country folks were abuzz over UFO sightings. The party line hummed, as upright citizens who would never get near LSD or Schnapps would recount, in church so it had to be true, stories of UFO sightings. If Old Roy Brenner said he saw a UFO, then UFOs were a matter of fact, and not just the fodder of a conspiracy theorist. Old Roy Brenner would never be arrested for being a conspiracy theorist. The only time he ever got in trouble with the law was for driving too slow. He's the reason for minimum speed limits in Kansas. Even Amish buggies passed Old Roy on his way to church.

The three girls, *those-most-highly-favored-among-men-and-angels*, were sleeping in The Cabin and we used baling wire to anchor us to the top of The Shed to keep from rolling off. Jeff, our field general, posed a curious question that roused us from our slumber: I wonder if we can hit The Cabin from here with a rock?

We cut ourselves loose from the baling wire and crawled down the lattice at the corner of the garage. Yes, that same lattice that we were NOT supposed to crawl up or down. A triangular appendage at the front corners of the garage, they started narrow at the ground level, then widened to two-feet in the eight-foot vertical span; they looked like ladders. Dad created them as artistic pieces to adorn our little garage on the prairie but we boys made the case that real art included both form and function; if it looked like a ladder then it should be climbed like a ladder.

We shimmied down the lattice, grabbed a few small rocks, and climbed back on The Shed. Sure enough, we could hit the cabin. After pelting it a few times, the girls hollered at us and asked if we were the ones making the racket.

We learned early to deny and make counteraccusations. We told them they were hearing things, wondered why they woke us up from our deep slumber, and barked at them to get back to bed.

Had we boys been the sharpest saws in the toolbox, it would have dawned on us that the Commander-in-Chief, his Secretary of War, and the Three Generals were sleeping inside the house with their windows open. They, of course, could only hear our male voices, not *those-most-highly-favored-among-men-and-angels*. We would have done well to heed Napoleon's wartime admonition not to wake up China because, once you did, the sleeping giant would devour all.

Like all wars that escalate, ours reached a feverish pitch when Jeff employed the trusted battlefield tactic of diversion; he yelled that he spotted a UFO. Jeff was the oldest and strongest, so Kendall and I followed him like any good lemming running into the sea. If he claimed he saw a UFO, then by Jove, we all saw a UFO. Bored little country kids have an intense imagination that leads them to frequently end up at the altar during the call to repentance.

Over forty years later, I remember being much braver that night than for which I stand accused in family folklore today. Yes, I was the first to reach the lattice, but I reasoned that I was going to run to The Cabin and save the girls. A gallant lad I was, my gentlemanly nature on display even in adolescence.

Poor little Kendall. He was the youngest and more vulnerable to trauma. Jeff bailed, I bailed, but Kendall was paralyzed on The Shed, a wailing mass of hormones so over stimulated by his hypothalamus that he didn't know whether to fight, flee, or wet himself, so he just stood there blubbering.

By this time we had all moved from the early stages of stationary panic into running-faster-than-a-speeding-bullet stage of panic. The girls were screaming, Kendall was crying, I was calling the Sherriff, and Jeff was screaming, "they're coming closer!"

Then the Commander-in-Chief and the Secretary of War woke up. From deep in the bowls of Command Central, we heard the Secretary roar out the open-window something about boys and noise and beatings and *for-crying-out-loud-do-you-know-what-time-it-is*.

The Commander-in-Chief was also the spiritual father of the clan that was part Scottish, part Irish, and three snorts Schnapps. By the time I came along – the last of six kids – age and perceived failure of raising my other five siblings had mellowed him. But this night, he stormed out of the house and hollered, "Well, Judas Priest!" In my Dad's world, that was as close to cursing and blasphemy as he ever got; the grass died where he spit that night.

We boys were marched off to the Siberian concentration camps after that to spend the rest of the summer in hard labor on a chain gang. We kept praying the UFO would show back up; we were ready to be captured.

Crawdaddin' in Bird Creek

T he best part of growing up in Kansas is the creeks, ponds, and swimming holes, all of which posed serious threats to our mortality. We didn't need violent video games; we defied death in real life.

In addition to sharing Hobson's Pond with the cows, we also had our version of the Amazon River: Bird Creek. The main difference between Hobson's Pond and Bird Creek was water quality. The cows turned Hobson's Pond toxic with their poor hygiene. They also justified ownership through eminent domain and argued that possession was 9/10ths of the law. Long before cows started drawing signs for Chik-fil-A, the cows of Hobson's Pond placed crude signs about the pasture that read:

- Boyz r stoopid

- Pond iz 4 cowz only

15

- We don't pee in your bathtub, don't pee in ours

- We can outrunn u

- Boyz pee when cows chase them

- Eat more boyz

However, Bird Creek was spring fed and scissoring through pastureland so the water was unusually clear for Kansas. Most cricks, er creeks, and rivers in Kansas are usually the color of a YourBucks latte and cause fish to glow in the dark and walk upright.

We frequented Bird Creek to fill 55-gallon barrels with water for our livestock. The well at our house was so pitiable it could only fill the bathtub with three inches of water. Saturday night baths were *high-time-on-the-farm* for everyone else but me. I was the youngest so I bathed last in shared bathwater. I might as well have bathed in Hobson's Pond.

Dad loaded two 55-gallon barrels in the bed of the pickup and we all jumped in the back without the slightest thought of seatbelts; they weren't even a law yet. Once we arrived at Bird Creek, Dad backed the pickup down so the tailgate was even with the water, then we'd get grab buckets to fill up the barrels and dump water on each other. We were boys; it was in our DNA.

To my recollection, we never skinny-dipped in Bird Creek. Although we did every other pond and stream for miles around, we never did Bird Creek for two reasons:

1. The water wasn't very deep

2. Crawdads are carnivores and attracted to worm-like things that wriggle in the water

There must be something primeval within a boy's DNA that each time they near an open body of water, they go skinny-dipping. If you ever stumble upon a bunch of boys in a pond or a good swimming hole in a creek, assume they are naked. When one swims

16

naked, they are far less likely to have a tiny bullhead catfish swim up their shorts and poke their poisonous barbs into one's manhood (or boyhood as it were-there's a story about that, too).

Girls, on the other hand, didn't seem to possess this biological urge to swim in their birthday suits. Try as we might, we could never convince the girls to join us. Oh, sure, they'd sneak up and steal our clothes or go home and rat us out, but they never joined in our reindeer games. Never.

Back to the crawdad: we loved crawdaddin'. Our favorite tactic was to string a ten-foot seine between us, trail a five-gallon bucket behind, and head up the creek. We'd walk several yards, swing the seine to the creek bank and haul out a catch of crawdads, perch, and the occasional water snake. In our honey-holes, there might be a hundred crawdads in each haul of the net. Some were so tiny and cute that we would let them dangle from our fingers pinching as hard as they could. But the big old 'dads had Yosemite Sam-like tempers and were ready to hurt someone. As soon as they came out of the water they started shooting off their mouths and taunting us.

If cows are the gossipy little old ladies of the animal kingdom, crawdads are the surly teenage boy bullies with zits and B.O. They have beady little Joe Biden eyes, disproportionately large pincers with which they strut around, and tattoos that signify gang membership. Get near a fish in the water and they swim away; get near a crawdad and they provoke a fight. Their usual tactics were to call us girly names, pinch us unmercifully in the softest tissue they could find and say bad things about our mammas.

One area of the creek had too many big rocks so a seine didn't work, but there were huge crawdads so we'd tie a piece of bacon to a string, lower it gently by a big rock, and let the crawdads pinch the bacon. We'd slowly ease it to the surface, reach our hand behind the crawdad's head, then quickly grab it with our index finger and thumb. However, if you open your index finger and thumb, it exposes that tender spot in-between and that's where they'd grab us. My father called our reaction *bellowing-like-a-bull-moose*.

The Cows of Hobson's Pond

The cows were right; boys are stoopid. They have a masochistic desire to prove virility by testing limits of pain with self-inflicted contrivances. We were too young yet to say *Hey, hold my beer and watch this!* while we launched into some death-defying dare, but we prepped for our teen years by tempting fate in other moronic ways.

Girls apparently don't have a desire to test their limits of pain like boys. I doubt we'll ever see a *Janeass* movie starring women because, well, they are a whole lot smarter than boys. Their form of self-flagellation was to read *Seventeen.*

On the list of *let's-see-how-much-this-hurts* activities such as sticking our tongues to frozen aluminum ice cube trays or shooting each other at point-blank range with rubber band guns, we decided to add one more brainless activity: how long can you let a granddaddy crawdad hang from your nipple by his pincer.

Suffice it to say I lost the contest. Even though I thought I was dying, I let him live out of respect as a worthy adversary.

My sons and I are now teaching my grandsons how to crawdad. They're toddlers unscathed by testosterone and a bit freaked out with all those swarming creatures in net. I walk through Bird Creek and wonder if that old crawdad is still alive. I'll bet he is and he's regaled his grandkids around the campfire with stories about the time he made a little boy cry. The big jerk.

I'll bet he's given them advice about picking fights, calling names, and has already instructed them: "If one of those little McNary boys ever catch you, just look him in the eye and whisper, 'Your granddad only lasted five seconds; think you can last ten?'"

I'll try to warn my grandsons. Doubt they'll listen once the testosterone kicks in.

Little Old Ladies of the Partyline Society

We country kids invented LOLOPS long before LOL (laugh out loud). LOLOPS: Little Old Ladies of the Partyline Society. We called them the Lollipops.

Unlike city folks that live so close they can hear each other pass gas, rural neighbors live miles apart. When we say, *Yeah, I grew up next to them*, it means we lived in the same county.

The community thread connecting neighbors was the Partyline, a shared phone line between neighbors, not the dogma of the Communist Party. One had to be careful to make that distinction if you didn't want to show up on Sen. McCarthy's or the Lollipop's list of Communist Sympathizers.

If you wanted to make a phone call on the Partyline, you picked up the receiver and listened in to make sure no one was talking before you dialed. It enraged the Lollipops if you started dialing while they were talking.

A distinctive click alerted you that someone picked up the phone. Whoever was gossiping, er, talking would stop, listen, then ask who joined the call: "Helen, is that you?" If it were my mom, Helen, she joined the gossip then hung up two hours later; Mom was a *bona fide* Lollipop. However, if one of us kids picked up the phone, we'd wet ourselves and run outside as fast as we could.

When the phone rang, you had to make sure it was your ring before you answered it. Ours was two short rings. Greenwell's was one long ring. One old man in the 'hood decided to answer it no matter whose ring it was.

My sister from back east kept calling to tell the folks she'd be a few days late, but the old man kept answering our ring. She finally made the old codger jump in the car and drive to our house to deliver the message. Carrier pigeons from New York would have been faster than that old geezer; the old man I mean, not my sister.

Long distance calls were only made in the case of an extreme emergency like when the Russians finally attacked. Our number was: 321-5067. Only you never said *three-two-one, five-o-six-seven*: you said, *Davis one, five-o-six-seven*. If you did make a long distance phone call, you called the operator first then had her dial the number. She often listened in to the call. I am not kidding.

You also called the operator if, say, someone was breaking into your house and you wanted to call the sheriff or if you just whacked off body parts with a chainsaw and needed an ambulance. But first, you interrupted the Partyline by declaring, "This is an emergency! I really need to call the operator so I can call the Sheriff."

However, one first had to be vetted by the Lollipops. They asked why you needed to call the sheriff then chatted a while about the times they called the sheriff. Sooner or later they decided whether or not you really needed to call the sheriff, but by that time, you didn't need to because the robbers took everything, including your phone.

Most of the gossipers on the party line were bored little old ladies. This was in the era when women stayed home and tormented their children. Several ladies on our Partyline managed to run their children off so they had nothing better to do than watch General Hospital and talk about the miscreants in the area; namely, the McNary children. The Lollipops was a clandestine society complete with secret handshakes, code words, late-night meetings with coal-oil lamps and Ouija boards. We lived in total fear of them.

My next older brother, Mike, was a cross between Gandalf and Gollum. He was wise and magical at times, then bad-tempered and dangerous at others. I lived in that dark chasm between abject terror and hero worship. Being the youngest of six and not in the original family strategic plan, I came along later after Mom and Dad thought they were done. I vehemently argued they saved the best for last, but my older brothers claimed I was a mistake and should have been born wearing rubber booties.

Mike finally cracked the code on the Lollipops. He worked for an electronics business and brought home a speakerphone that was the size of a toaster. This was *high excitement on the farm*! Remember, transistor radios were the pinnacle of technology during that time.

The idea was to take the phone of the hook, place the receiver in the cradle, and chat away doing whatever you wanted while you talked on the speakerphone. I am not making this up; the cover on the box was a photo of a lady ironing while she talked. My mother thought this was a marvelous idea; she could talk all day while ironing Dad's underwear. I am not making that up either.

Long before the NSA figured out how to spy on our cell phone calls, Mike figured out how to spy on the Lollipops. If you unscrewed the mouthpiece on the phone, the person on the other end couldn't hear what you were saying. Mike unscrewed the mouthpiece, laid the phone on the apparatus, and the Lollipops began questioning:

"Who just picked up the phone?"

Silence.

"Gertrude, did you just hear a click? I thought I heard a click. You sure you didn't hear a click?"

"Why yes, May Belle, I'm sure I heard a click, too. Did someone pick up the phone? Please identify yourself?"

Silence.

"Well, it was probably them darn McNary kids." Gertrude fumed, "they're as worthless as tits on a boar hog anyway."

"You know how them preacher's kids are. Their Daddy's a preacher and he's a good man but them kids of his is a sinnin' all week long and it wears him plumb out. He's got patches on his knees from praying for those little heathens!"

Have I told you yet my Daddy was a preacher? Well, that's a whole 'nother set of stories.

We were pretty darn cute listening in to the Lollipops until they bought up the topic of mountain lions eating some of the local rancher's calves. Solomon said that *too much knowledge brings sorrow*. However, he should have said that *too much knowledge scares the crap out of little kids.*

We had enough goblins to fear such as cows, coyotes, my niece Colleen and hateful crawdads; we didn't need to add mountain lions to the mix. The UFO coming to get us was an isolated moment of terror that could be reasoned away during daylight, but roaming mountain lions made us keep a Daisy Rider with us at all times. No one in the War Department trusted the rank-and-file with live ammo.

In the 40 years since we eavesdropped on the Lollipops, I've heard the Kansas Department of Wildlife and Parks deny, deny and deny again that there are mountain lions in Kansas. Even if you have a picture with a mountain lion eating your leg near your mailbox to verify the address, they quote the old Groucho Marx line, *you going to believe me or your lying eyes*? Naturally, I believe everything the government tells me.

On the other hand, I know people that I would trust much further than I can throw a government official say they've seen mountain lions in Kansas. I believe them.

I'm still not sure why we were surprised each time our espionage plans backfired. We laid a lot of traps as children and got caught in all of them, eaten by the same prey we tried to snare. Not one more night on the shed or in a tent was spent during our Kansas summers without the expectation of being eaten by mountain lions. Those lions would have found our young, hairless bodies nice, tasty lollipops.

It took us a lot of years and foiled plans to learn this lesson: never, ever, try to outsmart a little old lady. They'll always win even when they don't know they're playing a game.

The Cows of Hobson's Pond

The Day We Burned Old Man Leonard's Pasture

To get the flavor of growing up as country kid from Kansas, you should add *sauntering down a country road in the back of a pickup truck* to your bucket list. It should not matter to you that it is illegal. And, at some point, you need to add *pick-em-up* truck to your vocabulary since that's what our Missouri neighbors call them.

Although some folks think that riding in a convertible produces the same *wind-blowing-hair-in-your-face* type of excitement, they are sadly mistaken. Nothing compares to riding in the back of a pickup and yelling snide remarks at cows grazing by the fence. Since we dared not yell at the cows in Hobson's Pasture who ended up chasing us home each time, the protection of the pickup empowered us to insult the cows with reckless abandon.

25

The Cows of Hobson's Pond

Discretion is the better part of valor.

There are numerous things we did as kids that could have maimed or killed us which is why we've all grown up to be well-adjusted adults. Chief among our unwritten codes was this; *if the pickup is leaving the driveway and we can go, we are riding in the back.* Seatbelts, schmeatbelts; we defied common sense as often as we could. Long before Big Brother decided to make it the law to wear seatbelts, we rode in the back of pickup.

Unless you're a teenager out on a date, boredom quickly strikes a little kid in the back of a pickup. We'd make it about a hundred yards down the road and start looking for something to throw out. The girls seldom rode along leaving us without that option, so we'd stockpile rocks to throw at signs. On one occasion, we brilliantly decided to take firecrackers and toss them out the back.

Firecrackers in the 1960's were lethal. Long before attorneys started suing anything that breathes, you could get enough TNT at the Maynard's Bait Stand to blow up a small Buick. Consequently, I was instructed by my Mom to *never light a firecracker in your hand and throw it, you little dingbat, or you'll blow your fingers off.*

I grew up with punitive justice swiftly meted out by either Mom or God, so I had a healthy fear of lighting a firecracker and throwing it. Naturally, my nephew Jeff (who was a year older than me) helped me overcome this fear by regularly checking my dipstick for testosterone levels. *Come on*, he would say, *it's fun*, he would say, *it won't hurt you*, he would say, *don't be a sissy*, he would say. Jeff was to me what the serpent in the Garden of Eden was to Eve.

One hot July day, Dad loaded up the 55-gallon drums in the back of the pickup and hollered at us to jump in. Hot dang, it was time to go crawdaddin' on Bird Creek! We never once thought of getting in the front, so we'd pile in the back and settle in for the ride. Only this time we had firecrackers and a punk. I have often wondered why firecracker lighters are called punks other than they are named after the idiots holding them.

We were forbidden to throw anything out while we were on Highway 54, but as soon as we turned onto the graveled road, every projectile we could scrape up started sailing. Only this time it wasn't rocks, it was firecrackers. Dad did not have the same rule that Mom did about *never light a firecracker in your hand and throw it, you little dingbat, or you'll blow your fingers off.* Dad intuitively knew we needed a fair amount of risk in our lives to make us wholesome adults.

After I grew up and had kids of my own, I waited until they got older before I trusted their capacity to reason with me. Little kids are not rational beings; they don't understand cause-and-effect. It doesn't matter how many times you tell a child not to stick the fork in the electrical outlet, they won't believe you until they fry themselves a couple of times.

We obviously lacked these reasoning skills or it would have occurred to us that, on a hot July day in Kansas, you don't throw things with shooting sparks on dry grass. The pastures were as explosive as a Joe Pesci getting the wrong order at a McDonalds drive-thru.

We made it to Bird Creek, filled the drums up with water for our critters back home, then commenced to crawdaddin'. I was tempting a big ol' crawdad under a rock with a piece of bacon tied to a string when the big water truck pulled up. The driver jumped out and threw a hose in our creek to suck up water.

"Hey Bill!" my Dad said. "How you doing?"

"Hi Bob, just needing a little water. The pasture up the road is on fire."

They chatted above the din of the engine sucking water out of precious honey-hole and totally ruined our crawdaddin' for the day. We were not impressed. Bill finally topped of the huge tank on the back of the truck, ground a few gears and raced off to fight the fire.

"Hey boys," Dad said. "Want to go fight a fire?"

Does a bear poop in the woods? What a silly question; of course we wanted to go fight a fire! Adventure! Intrigue! Danger! Romance! Okay, well, maybe not romance since we hadn't hit puberty, but we instinctively knew that one day soon reciting stories of dangerous encounters would woo the ladies. One day, puberty would finally sit in and totally screw up our value system.

We jumped in the back of the pickup and puttered up the road to the fire. Several water trucks raced across the prairie shooting out plumes of water on the line of fire, neighbors came from miles around with grain shovels and gunny sacks, and the sheriff deputies cordoned off the road with lights flashing.

The pasture belonged to Old Man Leonard who we feared about as much as we did the Russians (this was during the Cold War). Old Man Leonard lived in a haunted house that hadn't been painted or had the windows washed since the Great Depression. Looking back, I often wonder where the fear came from because none of us ever had an encounter with him; it was more like a *hair-standing-on-the-back-of-your-neck* feeling. We'd see his skinny American Gothic body in bib-overalls carrying a shovel and we assumed it was to bury children. Remember that part I said about not reasoning with children? This is why.

We ripped off our shirts, dipped them in a water barrels and raced out to the pasture to fight the raging inferno. Now, in the springtime in the Flint Hills, the ranchers intentionally light pastures on fire at night when the wind is calm; it is a thing of beauty. But, during a hot summer day when the wind is blowing like the exhaust out of a jet engine, a pasture fire is something to fear. A summer pasture fire can move faster than paparazzi chasing George Clooney.

The fire was finally conquered and it was time to shake hands, swap exaggerated tales, compare this fire to the one back in '53 that traveled 35 miles in two hours, and hand out awards to the bravest firefighters of the day.

We won the award for bravery in the face of grave danger. Sprite youth formerly despised by Old Man Leonard were suddenly thrust into great favor from pauper to prince. Former feelings of fear and hostility abated, peace offerings were extended, land was offered for our exploration, and iced tea passed out to thirsty heroes. It was a glorious day.

As we crawled in the back of the pickup enjoying a collective sense of pride hitherto unknown to our little tribe of miscreants, Dad leaned against the side of the truck and dropped the bomb, "You boys do realize, don't you, that you're the ones that set that pasture on fire?"

We waved at Old Man Leonard as we puttered off down the road with our soot-covered bodies being splashed with water sloshing out of the 55-gallon drums. We smiled like politicians but trembled in fear like feverish skunks. It's a sick feeling to think you're a hero only to find out you're the criminal.

Mom was right; I was a dingbat. By the time the summer was over I managed to hang on to a firecracker too long. I retained all the digits in my right hand, but not without some serious blood blisters. After the firecracker detonated, I ran upstairs and lay in bed hoping I would die before Mom discovered me. She finally discovered me whimpering under the covers and assured me that my mangled fingers were not the punishment of God; they were the just rewards for being a dingbat.

You would have thought I would have learned my lesson. But I've managed to stick the fork in the electrical outlet a few more times since then. All of that experience added a certain *gravitas* when I relayed helpful information to my own children: *never light a firecracker in your hand and throw it, you little dingbat, or you'll blow your fingers off.*

The Cows of Hobson's Pond

Fear- the Fastest Form of Transportation

The first time I got in trouble for exploring, I threw the family dog under the bus. Wanderlust took over my little four-year-old mind and I grabbed the dog, Boo-Boo, and headed out across the pasture. Mom alerted the Lollipops (Little Old Ladies of the Partyline Society) that I was missing and they called all the neighbors to rendezvous at the McNary house to look for that stupid little kid. Someone soon spotted my head bobbing in the ravine in the pasture a hundred yards from the house and I was rescued. When quizzed, I responded, "Wasn't me. Boo-Boo made me do it." I learned early the power to deny and make counter accusations.

In the early '60's, parents didn't live in total fear of child abduction like they do nowadays. When the Lollipops sent out the Mayday signal, not one person thought I'd been kidnapped. Eaten, maybe, but not kidnapped. Mountain lions, coyotes, or cows might have got me, but not a two-legged critter. The cows were always

31

suspects in anything that had to do with the torment of little children, but they were at least honest when interrogated. They happily confessed to inflicting physical and mental harm on our young souls.

In those days, our parents booted us out the door in summer as soon as the breakfast dishes were done. Even on good days they didn't let us back in until dinner. That was okay; we didn't want to go back inside anyway; the Generals hung out in the Command Center and nothing good happened in there that concerned us little kids.

Although the aforementioned escapade with Boo-Boo was before my memory bank started storing things in the *gee-that-was-fun-let's-do-it-again* vault, I've always had a desire to explore.

A desire to explore is a mixture of curiosity, mischief, danger, and mayhem. If you can't get hurt then you're not exploring. If that rock doesn't have the chance of a venomous viper coiled ready to lunge, then you're not exploring. If that cave doesn't have bootleggers ready to chop you up in little pieces, then you're not exploring. If pirates can't make you walk the plank on Hobson's Pond, then you're just goofing off. Exploring has to involve varying degrees of pain.

We created various categories of explorers. See where you fit.

Whiny Butt Explorers: Although we weren't allowed to say the word *butt,* the Whiny Butt Explorer commenced grumbling at the first suggestion of *let's-go-exploring*! They came up with more objections than federal regulators about why it was *too cold* or *too hot* or *too many bugs* or *gee-I-could-lose-my-legs*. Whiny Butt Explorers grew up to be Discovery Channel devotees who watch shows about the Amazon and suddenly become experts on the jungle. But one glimpse of their soft hands and tender underbellies lets you know the riskiest adventure they embark on is Black Friday shopping.

Mickey Mouse Club Explorers: These lucky ducks stumble

on buried treasure by accident while planting trees for Arbor Day. They really aren't explorers, but they discover the bounty for which explorers search. Then the Mickey Mouse Explorers march right out and buy an Indiana Jones hat and bullwhip. We loathed them and made fun of their hats until they bought us ice cream.

He-Man-Woman-Haters Explorers: Like the Little Rascals club of the same name, their curiosity is about one degree warmer than their fear. They nervously lift up rocks looking for snakes; they get stuck in caves and bloat like a toad gorging on June bugs; they go coon hunting in the dark with a 100K watt floodlight strapped to each arm and one on the head. I've done each of these. The HMWH explorer is a conflicted person often conned by a Daniel Boone Explorer or, heaven forbid, a Mount Everest Explorer. They splurge on exploring books, then splurge on exploring, then splurge on therapists or medical doctors to heal whichever wound is most life-threatening.

Daniel Boone Explorers: They've done their research, poured over the maps, then wander off believing they have a strong chance of returning home alive and relatively unscathed. Other than having to wrestle bears on occasion, they've stacked the odds in their favor and know they will live another day to explore. They might have a few bullet holes in their coonskin caps, but their scalps are still intact. Daniel Boone Explorers instill confidence in followers with well-narrated stories of adventure.

Mount Everest Explorers: These are the die-hard adrenaline junkies who, by the time they are forty, have broken every bone in their body and go through snakebite kits like they're M&M's. Mount Everest Explorers are best admired from a distance. If you get too close, they will suck you into their adventure screaming like a cat with its tail slammed in the door. Mount Everest Explorers often end up being boiled in pots by cannibals.

One day my nephew Kendall and I decided to explore unchartered territory. We poured over maps, checked weather conditions then pointed our Zebco 202's east and trekked to a pond in the middle of untamed pasture where we expected large fish to be waiting on us. This pasture seemed less dangerous than Hobson's Pasture because none of our mortal enemies, the cows, lived there. Hobson's Cows spotted us leaving and rushed to the fence to offer encouragement and advice.

"Hey," Marge mooed, "come on back this way. We promise we won't chase you this time."

"No," I defied her, "you told us that the last time and I still have scratches on my back from diving under the barbwire to get away from you."

"Well, suit yourself," Gertrude sneered, "You're going to die anyway. There's rattlesnakes in that pasture."

Hobson's Cows were more annoying than Kanye West at the Grammys.

The new pasture was more difficult to navigate because no cows had eaten or tromped the grass so it was a veritable jungle of tall grass and weeds. Neither the Generals nor the Commander-in-Chief trusted us with sharp objects like machetes so we barehanded it through the prairie jungle with our Zebco 202 fishing poles held high.

Either the fish saw us coming with our Prince Albert can of worms or the cows had telepathically warned them to go into submarine mode and *run silent, run deep*, because our bobbers never showed a nibble. Not even the chubbiest night crawler dancing like Little Richard could get a rise out of the catfish inhabiting the murky depths.

We fished an interminably long time, at least fifteen minutes. Then we decided to go slashing back through the grass. About thirty feet into the grass I heard the distinct sound of a rattlesnake; those dumb cows were right.

I hadn't learned to cuss yet or I would have said that word that describes what you do in your underwear when your ten-years-old and hear a rattlesnake. The wind was blowing hard enough to rustle the grass so my little mind tried to ration that it was just the grass but then… OH CRAP, THE COWS WERE RIGHT, THAT'S A RATTLSNAKE! To make things worse, I couldn't see it and since all reason had vacated my imaginative mind, I could not figure out where it was.

Little kids don't have much normal reasoning capacity anyway, but shoot a little fear-laced adrenaline in their veins and they turn into hyperventilating morons. We levitated like cartoon characters then shot off across the pasture running on the grass tops. Mel Brooks, in the interview with the 2,000 year-old-man, said it best: *fear is the fastest form of transportation.*

I could hear the other rattlesnakes giggling like a bunch twelve-year-old boys at an R-rated movie:

"Hey, Larry, you got them real good!" the mouthy one, Jimmy said. "Each time you rattled they trembled a little bit more! They shook more than our rattles! You scared them so bad they left their fishing poles behind, but what is that god-awful smell? Smells like someone, OH GROSS, I JUST SLITHERED IN IT."

Served him right.

Exploring is an adventure and an adventure is something you sit at home in your easy chair dreaming about. However, when you're out having an adventure, you wish you were sitting at home in your easy chair.

All this writing about adventure has me itching to go explore. I'm surrounded by acres and acres of wide-open country in Kansas, I think I'll lace up the hiking boots and start walking. I should be okay. It's still winter, and the rattlesnakes are hibernating. But I think I'll traipse down the old abandoned railroad bed instead of thru the pasture full of cows. I'm too darn slow to outrun them anymore.

The Cows of Hobson's Pond

Passing Gas in Church

One dare not laugh in the little country church I grew up in or some little old lady would accuse you of sinning. Church was a somber place where the virtues of God competed with the vices of the devil and the devil seemed to be winning; we were supposed to feel bad about that. The French philosopher Voltaire believed *cogito, ergo, sum* (I think, therefore I am). However, my Mom believed *culpa, ergo, sum* (I'm guilty, therefore I am).

One rarely laughed in church because, well, God doesn't laugh because everyone is going to *hell-in-a-hand-basket* and that ain't nothin' to laugh about. After all, *you might get ran over by a car while crossing a street after church* so the last thing you want before meeting your Maker is to defile the holy of holies by laughing.

St. Peter: "So, Rick, you thought Mrs. Kennedy falling asleep then having her dentures fall out was funny?"

Me: "Oh, no, St. Peter, I was actually crying because I felt sorry for her, not because I was laughing."

St. Peter: "Nice. Not only did you laugh in church but now you're lying about it, too. It's no wonder *you got ran over by a car while crossing a street after church.*

Like Pavlov's dogs salivating when the bell is rung, I developed a morose tendency to laugh during the most unsuitable times. I blame it on my upbringing; the devil makes me do it.

However, even though we weren't supposed to laugh, we catalogued various kinds of laughter.

The Snicker: It was okay to snicker at a lame joke Dad told for the umpteenth time. We kids sat bored out of ever-loving minds on the back row of the west section of pews. We hid Louis L'amour books in our Bibles and acted as pious as little heathens can. The 5-Star General- my Mom- sat about halfway up the east section with a couple of her little old lady friends; a brood you might call them.

Mom was our barometer for The Snicker. If she snickered, we snickered. When she snickered she turned like an owl spinning its head to make sure we were snickering, too. We obliged so we could get an ice cream cone later.

The Chuckle: This laugh was a response to something Dad said that was accidentally funny. He didn't mean for it to be funny, but he would tangle his tongue and turn the *fiery darts of Satan* into the *diery farts of Satan.* Of course, we all had to quickly repent of having fun lest we'd *get ran over by a car while crossing a street after church.*

The Chortle: This was reserved for a guest speaker that was actually funny. One missionary told great jokes about cannibals and gave us hope that we weren't all going to hell on a grease-covered slipper slide. If one could tell a good cannibal joke, one was assured a devoted following by the back-row boys at our little country church. The next missionary with the hateful marimba-playing wife would have done well to include cannibal jokes in his arsenal.

The Snort: This was caused by another kid or by Old Roy Brenner. Old Roy's eyebrows were so bushy it looked like a gray squirrel died and left his tail on Roy's forehead. Old Roy was a crotchety old guy that started complaining as soon as he walked in the door; we loved him because he annoyed the little old ladies thereby making himself the object of their scorn, not us.

Furthermore, Roy introduced us boys - right there in church- to the first naked female breast we ever saw that wasn't crossed out with magic markers in a National Geographic. We were lost somewhere on the trail with Louis L'amour when he snorted and motioned with his eyebrows to look across the way; a lady with a dozen kids was nursing. She was not a bit bashful about having her buffet line and silverware on display both before and after her little diners filled their bellies. Naturally, our young minds were piqued with scientific curiosity so we sat staring like a deer-in-the-headlights. Old Roy's name is still mentioned with great reverence.

The Snort could be contained if you inverted your hands and pinched your nose between your little fingers and stuck your thumbs in your ears. Usually, we could keep it under wraps until someone start giggling again and you felt the pew tremble. But the Snort was as combustible to the brain as a 2-liter 7-Up bottle stuffed full of Mentos and, once it escaped, sounded like an elephant sneeze. You could go to the bathroom and get a Snort under control until you came back and the pew startled trembling again.

Then there was **The Wheeze.** A Wheeze meant you just got up and walked out of church thinking that if you got *ran over by a car while crossing a street after church*, you'd die a happy boy.

Wednesday nights were pretty low-key in our little country church. The adults sat on the east side and the kids sat on the west side. The girls grew weary of getting in trouble because of us boys so they moved. We boys staked our claim on the back row and the girls set up camp in the front. Life was good.

We were in our typical catatonic state but on our best behavior because we wanted to go to Dairy Queen afterward. We lived by the beatitude, *blessed are those who behave themselves, for they shall get an ice cream cone after church.*

One of the worst things a public speaker can do to an audience is to say *in closing* and not mean it. To this day, if someone says *in closing*, I last about 30 seconds. Again, it's a Pavlovian response. Dad was notorious for tormenting us this way. Dad finally closed his remarks and told us all to bow heads and close our eyes; God only listens if your eyes are closed.

Half-way through the prayer, a Gatling gun of flatulence erupted from the young girls section which, that night, was occupied by just two girls. We had enjoyed Tommy Orton's chili for school lunch that day and apparently various parts of digestive system of one young lady declared war on each other. Gastrointestinal combat raged inside her as battle lines were drawn and each side rumbled tanks into place as they jockeyed for position. Then one crazed soldier finally launched an offensive and shot off a round of rapid-fire retorts that were so loud we expected heavy artillery to follow.

Dad stopped dead in his tracks. We boys jerked our heads up to see if we could tell which of the dainty damsels had spontaneously combusted. Soon the mystery was revealed as one young lady yelled at the other one, "Oh my gosh, Alice, that smells awful!"

I don't know if Dad ever finished his prayer that night; we bolted for the door like someone zapped us with a cattle prod. We collapsed in the snow, wheezing for air, and did not care if we *did get ran over by a car while crossing a street after church.* If we did, we would die in as rich of bliss as any prepubescent boy has ever enjoyed.

Being good predestination Calvinists, we couldn't help but conclude that this was God's will for our lives. As the Good Book says, *all things work together for good to those who love the Lord.* I can't help but thinking God thought it was funny, too, but I doubt if St. Peter grills God like I anticipate being grilled.

It turns out *we didn't get ran over by a car while crossing a street after church that night.* We got an ice cream cone instead.

How I Learned to Detest the Marimba

I didn't always detest the marimba; I had help. I blame it all on a traveling Evangelist and his marimba-playing wife.

My Dad worked in the oilfields but his real passion was to minister to a small country church he built with his own hands. He never took any pay and the church sent any leftover money to missionaries around the world.

As a result, the missionaries we supported occasionally came to speak in our church. All of these people gave up comfort in America to risk their lives taking the good news of the love of God to the jungles of South America or to sneak Bibles behind the Iron Curtain. I loved the missionaries.

We adored one missionary because he told cannibal jokes. There are few things little boys on the back row of church love more than cannibal jokes. He also told scary stories about the jungles of South America that kept me awake for three nights in a row. He was a friend of the five martyred missionaries documented in the movie, "End of the Spear."

However, the traveling evangelists were another story. They were supposed to be sharing the good news of the love of God, too, but mostly they scared the living daylights of people. I was 43 years old before I heard an Evangelist that didn't make me wet my pants in fear.

Whereas missionaries came to give a report; Evangelists came to *make people git right with God*. Missionaries felt called to share the love of God in the most primitive conditions imaginable; Evangelists felt called to drink Dad's coffee, eat Mom's cherry pie, and bellyache about us kids. Missionaries stayed a day or two; Evangelists stayed a week. Evangelists lived up to Dad's axiom that *guests are like fish; after three days they begin to stink.*

Evangelists held week-long revival meetings at our church which meant the pulpit took a particularly vigorous beating that week. Guilt and fear were their main themes, and most lived by the motto *"read the Bible; it will scare the hell out of you"*.

The Evangelist's goal was to pack people to the altar at the end of the service for rededication or repentance. Naturally, the best way to make people repent is to scare the hell out of them or make them feel lower than worm poop. After all, you were likely to *get ran over by a car while crossing a street after church* so you better *git right with God.*

We didn't really have an altar; it was just a stage with a pulpit in the center, but it was symbolic of the holy of holies. The Evangelist wouldn't quit until *someone went forward to meet Jesus and git right with God.* This was a burning bush moment with Divine. Apparently Jesus didn't hang out on the back row with us little boys; you had to walk up front to meet him.

It was not uncommon for my little rear to get dragged to the altar during those visits because the religious interlopers would convince my folks that I was the spawn of the devil and I'd better repent or the whole house was going to hell in a hand basket. One couple convinced my folks that my *Leave it to Beaver* language like *darn, shoot, heck,* and *gee-whiz* meant I was cussing like a sailor. I was on the devil's side and would soon be sporting a bifurcated tail and brandishing a pitchfork.

The Evangelist would not quit until *someone went forward to meet Jesus and git right with God.* I won't name names, but I know a few folks who *went forward to meet Jesus* just so the Evangelist would shut up and we could head to Dairy Queen.

Revivals were about numbers. The number of people who attended, the number of people who converted to Christianity, the number of people who repented of all their sins to *git right with God,* and the number of dollars dropped in the collection plate for the evangelist.

One of the things I admired most about my Dad is that he finally quit passing the offering plate. Instead, he put a box in the back of the church and said *"If you want to give, give; if you don't want to give, don't give. Shoving a plate under your nose while the piano plays 'I Surrender All' is not a good reason to give; God loves a cheerful giver."* Surprisingly, contributions rose significantly after he stopped taking up an offering.

The Evangelist and the marimba-playing wife descended on our house in an old brown station wagon packed with the marimba and all its accouterments. As we settled in for a week-long series of hellfire-and-damnation sermons, I waited to see what new things I'd get in trouble for at home. It was always a crapshoot.

Mr. Evangelist knew it was about numbers, too, so he offered a contest: whoever invited the most people won a brand-spanking new leather-covered Bible.

Being the spiritually competitive person that I was, I invited all my friends from school who were pagans and backsliders. I told them about the exotic sounds of the marimba and how they were going to hell-in-a-hand basket and needed to come hear one of the greatest Evangelists of all time. I didn't bother telling them about the contest; I choose to obscure my selfish motives with righteous acts done for public recognition.

Each night, Dad opened up the service with a prayer and three hymns then turn it to over to the evangelist. The Evangelist rambled on about the contest and how awesome the marimba was and how fortunate we were to have his wife bless us with her skill. She always fussed around with the marimba while he was talking and acted like she was embarrassed by the accolades. She would flit coy glances his way like the mama bear saying to Bugs Bunny, *tell me more about my eyes.*

She would then attack the marimba like it had personally insulted her. I've watched marimba players with exquisite skill play as if they are one with the instrument, but this woman looked like she was on the giving end of spousal abuse.

Being a Muppet fan, I associated the marimba with calypso music so I expected lively *I'll Fly Away* or *Shoutin' in That Amen Corner* kind of music. What we got instead were dirges and dark renditions of Judgment Day Songs because *you're going to get run over in the street when you leave here tonight so you better come forward to meet Jesus and git right with God.*

The revival was drawing to a close on the last night and I was ahead in the numbers game. Hands down, I brought the greatest number of pagans and backsliders to the meetings. I was finally going to get my cherished prize.

Before Mr. Evangelist announced the winner, Mrs. Marimba walked over to him and whispered something in his ear. He rambled on for a bit about how good a week it had been, how many folks had *come forward to meet Jesus and git right with God* and how good the offerings had been and why he needed to come back soon. Real soon.

Then he dropped the bomb; the fine print in the contest said the competition for the brand-spanking new leather-covered Bible was only good for adults; kids were excluded.

I might not be the brightest crayon in the Crayola box, but I saw the lines in the coloring book well enough to conclude that Mrs. Marimba rigged the vote; she must have been from Florida.

Many years have passed and you will be happy to know I've repented and became a marimba-believer again. I *got right with the marimba* thanks to the Muppet's Marvin Suggs and the Muppahone.

Although the numbers from Mr. Evangelist and Mrs. Marimba were better than average, we never saw them in our church or home again.

However, the next Sunday in church, Dad called me to the front of the church. He made a comment about all the pagans and backsliders I brought the following week and how proud the church was of me then he gave me a brand-spanking new leather-covered Bible. He knew what it took to *git right with God.*

World Peace and a Good Old Kansas Swimmin' Hole

The best way to foster world peace is to get all the kings, queens, presidents, dictators and their hench-people together at a good ol' Kansas swimmin' hole. Putin could strut bare-chested in his Speedo; Merkel could hold the NSA director's head under water; Kim Jong Un could do cannonballs and splash everyone in reach; China would loan everyone money to buy trinkets at their kiosks; John Boehner could show off his fake-bake and everyone would hold ISIS's head under water until the bubbles stopped. I'm now probably on the black list of at least a half-a-dozen countries.

The best eight words we ever heard as kids were, *Load up! We're going to the swimmin' hole!* We'd drop everything, grab a couple of inner tubes, jump in the back of Dad's old pickup and putter down a graveled road to heaven on a creek bank.

Our swimmin' hole was a pool of water where Shady Creek widened under an old limestone arched bridge along Price Road. Shady Creek snuck through the pastures and wheat fields until it was the color of a mocha latte. It wound lazily through the pasture like a fat kid eating chips in front of a T.V. except during the spring rains when it screamed like me trying to outrun the cows in Hobson's Pasture.

Looking back, I divide my time in the Swimmin' Hole into two distinctive eras: before I had hair on my body, and after I had hair on my body.

Something dreadful happens when hair starts growing on a little boy's body; his perception of reality is altered. Truths about the female species he formerly held as self-evident and universal soon become suspect and relative. Former enemies- namely all members of the female species – now become someone for whom they will go great lengths to impress. Those same females whom they formerly regarded with contempt and scorn soon become cherished for every word they say and eye they bat.

Here are a few examples of this transformation:

Jumping Off the Bridge

The top of the arched bridge was 17 feet from the ledge to the water. To give you perspective, 17 *horizontal* feet is like the distance between a basketball goal and the free-throw line (actually, it's only 15 feet, but you get my drift). However, when you're ten years old, 17 *vertical* feet is like the distance between the top of the Chrysler Building and the street below.

Jumping off the bridge was an exhilarating activity that proved one's bravado to other male species. We jumped off the bridge into inner tubes, we jumped off the bridge trying to catch balls thrown at us, we jumped off the bridge beating our chest like Tarzan, and we jumped off the bridge doing cannonballs and can-openers.

We continued jumping until puberty took over; then we started diving. As the levels of testosterone elevated in our little bodies, the capacity to make reasonable decisions diminished proportionately; with each new hair that sprung up, dozens of brain cells died. Suddenly, jumping was not sufficient; we needed to dive.

The problem with diving off the bridge was that the water was too shallow. When we jumped off the bridge, we buckled our legs soon as we hit the water to provide a cushion when we hit the bottom. If we dived off, then we'd be like a torpedo headed straight to the rocks below and we would die.

However, we came up with a solution. The diver had to hit with water and immediately curve upward like a dolphin leaping out of water. Timing was critical because if you started too soon, well, the pain of belly-flop from 17 feet is excruciating.

Swimmin' with the Water Snakes

Before hair started growing on our little bodies, we lived in peaceful co-habitation with the water snakes that lived in the bushes on the south bank of the creek. We signed an MOU (*memorandum of understanding*) with them; the snakes were to *stay in the bushes* and we were to *stay away from the bushes*. This also insured that the girls who were our relatives wouldn't go swimming with us. On the off chance we arrived to find neighbor girls in our swimmin' hole, we immediately called their attention to the snakes. This cleared people out faster than a preacher walking into the local brothel on Saturday night.

But let a little hair start growing on our bodies and we suddenly wanted all the neighbor girls to go swimming. The three girls in our family heretofore unwanted now served a particularly useful purpose; they had friends they could bring along.

However, soon all the girls quit going because of the snakes. We called for a meeting with the snakes and asked if they would vacate the premises and move on downstream. Their Attorney

General, a defiant litigator who made his living defending serial killers, contended that they were there first and we had no right asking them to leave ancestral lands, er, waters.

Being good American citizens, we invoked historical precedents like Manifest Destiny, Eminent Domain, and the Just War Theory. Then we threatened them. Being snakes and doing what snakes do, they rallied their forces and slithered around the swimming hole until it looked like spaghetti boiling in water. Naturally, we shot at them with BB guns like an old gunslinger making a cowpoke dance. The cause and effect was what we predicted; the snakes disappeared and the girls returned.

Co-Ed Chicken Wars

Before hair started growing on our little bodies, the only reason to have physical contact with girls was to dunk them. We dunked them for two reasons: to make life unpleasant enough they would want to stay home next time, and to shut them up because they were annoying.

Much to our dismay, Dad wouldn't let us hold them under too long for fear the bubbles would stop. We knew that dunking them was going to result in punishment handed out later by the matriarchs – the Three Generals- but it was worth it. But as soon as the girls hit the back door of the house, they'd blab about being dunked. I'll have it be known that I never once tried to dunk my nemesis and niece, Colleen Miller. Others who tried dunking her walked around with a hitch in their git-a-long for the rest of their lives or found dead horse heads on their pillows at night.

However, after our body chemistry changed, we found the game of co-ed chicken wars exceedingly likeable. When we played chicken wars with another guy on top of our shoulders, the goal to end as quickly as possible so the result usually ended in carnage and name-calling. However, we discovered playing co-ed chicken wars with girls on our shoulders was far more pleasurable if we played it slowly so no one got injured.

Being experienced chicken war strategists, we boys determined that the girls needed a particular style of uniform, you know, to encourage morale, set one's self apart from others in battle, and be worn with the entire dignity incumbent upon a soldier-at-war. After a series of grueling product tests including fabric strength and camouflage design, we determined the most appropriate combat-ready uniform was (roll call, please): Daisy Duke shorts with a bikini top!

Many years later, I firmly believe that all the world's problems can be solved at a good ol' Kansas swimming hole. Congress could grab the mud off the bottom and literally sling it at each other; Israel and the Palestinians could have a *who-can-hold-their-breath-underwater-the-longest* contest; the African tribes could build a campfire on the evening shore and sing Kum-ba-yah.

And who knows, maybe all it would take for Kim Jong Un to take his itchy finger off his doomsday trigger is to see Queen Elizabeth in a pair of Daisy Duke shorts and a bikini top.

The Cows of Hobson's Pond

What I Learned in Second Grade About the Weaker Sex

Whomever said that females are the weaker sex did not learn the same lessons I did in second grade at my rural grade school: country girls are tough.

My first encounter with the weaker sex happened on the playground. Looking back on the kind of playground equipment we had, it's a small wonder we're not all missing body parts or walking with a limp. Where were the plastic slipper slides while we were blistering our bottoms on those old shiny metal ones? Where was the cushy matt to fall on when Pippi Longstocking pile-drived me off the merry-go-round then rolled me over and started kissing me? Where were the caps to cover the pipes that housed fourteen thousand wasps that terrorized little children? What's that? You want to know more about the incident with Pippi? Oh, sure, I talk about being wounded by playground equipment and all you want to know about is the first time I was molested by a girl.

My first, second, and third grade teacher were all the same person: Mrs. Beulah Bohn. Mrs. Bohn looked like Granny off the Beverly Hillbillies and was only two inches taller than the rest of us second-graders. Mrs. Bohn was the quintessential schoolmarm with the hem of her skirt way below her knees and black shoes with a low heel. Kansas's winters would not deny us our birthright of spending recess outside, so Mrs. Bohn would try to stay warm by hopping up and down like a robin. Other than Pippi attacking me, and Eugene Saunders starting a chain reaction of little kids barfing, that is about all I remember about a woman with whom I spent my first three years of formal education.

The situation in question happened one blustery day on the playground with dirt the consistency of concrete. Oh, sure, someone sprinkled a few grains of sand under the monkey bars to make it look like it would cushion the blow, but it didn't matter what playground equipment you were thrown from, the likelihood of breaking a bone was pretty high. To my recollection, no parent ever whined to the principal about the equipment because they didn't even have recess back in their day when they had to walk three miles to get to school.

I was minding my own business swirling around on the merry-go-round and decided to jump off. I was headed to the monkey bars to see if I could to knock the wind out of my lungs and the next thing I know, someone face plants me in the hard-pan. I *uuumphed* as the air was knocked out of me then I was violently rolled over on my back so my attacker could begin kissing me. She smelled a whole lot better than Eugene.

I did not have enough hair growing on my body yet to enjoy that moment for what it was. Later, though, I would not only regret having fought her off, I would offer chocolates and flowers to a variety of the female species in anticipation of being abused that away again.

As I was fighting off my attacker, Mrs. Bohn started hopping again. *"Rick,* she chirped, *you quit that! You leave Pippi alone!"*

Naturally, I was the one in trouble. Since I already learned the lesson from my nieces and the Three Generals that resided at our house during the summer that males are *always* guilty of *everything* that is wrong in the world, I immediately accepted the guilt and anticipated the punishment. Not much could be worse than getting kissed by a third-grader, but a few un-repented-of-sins came to mind so I concluded that I deserved it. I'd been marched to the principal's office for lesser crimes against humanity; surely this one was not worthy of the dreaded swats.

My other encounter with the weaker sex happened on the bus. As time passed, I decided the experience with Pippi hadn't been so bad after all; in fact, it was more enjoyable than I first realized. I thought I was dizzy from being pile-driven into the hard pan, but it turned out that my dizziness came from my little second-grade heart palpitating to a new stroke after being smooched. I concluded that the encounter was worth repeating and thus began my life-long quest to relive that moment with Pippi.

Candace Johnson was the prettiest girl in my class and we shared the same bus route. The bus route for rural schools is the devils workshop for stirring up unscrupulous ideas in the minds of *bored-out-of-your-gourd* little boys. Riding for an hour in the morning and an hour in the evening of largely unsupervised time is an opportunity to concoct various forms of mischief. Second-graders are still short enough to hide most of their activity from the omniscient eye of the bus driver that stared at you in a gigantic rearview mirror. However, we were still sent to the principal's office with great frequency to atone for sins committed on the bus route.

During my childhood, the school hired former Gestapo operatives planted in our community through a witness relocation program to be our bus drivers. Naturally, to hide their former identities as torturers and prison guards, they assumed surnames appropriate for our culture like Smith and Jones then dressed up as little old ladies with beehive hair-dos and bright red lipstick. They smiled knowingly when we referred to them as *Fraulein.* Regardless of how well they pulled off their disguises, in times of great rage at the little occupants on the bus, their thick German dialect revealed the origins of their motherland.

It was on one of those interminable bus routes that I decided to make my move on Candace. Since Pippi was so forthcoming with her affections for the male species, I assumed that all females were so inclined. Thus began my lifelong predilection of not understanding women. Furthermore, here's a good lesson for all adults: never trust the logic of a second grade boy that's just been kissed for his first time.

However, Candace was not thusly inclined and wanted a bribe of chocolates and roses first. Or at the very least, I was supposed to pass her a note and ask her to *please go out with me, check yes or no.* I'm not sure where we were supposed to go, but she was supposed *to go out with me* before I made my move.

It turned out that Candace had a mean right hook. She anticipated my amorous intention and, as I leaned in for the smooch, she feigned with her left then busted me in the nose with her right.

This was the second most valuable lesson I've learned about the female species: their instincts are uncanny. If the instinct of a woman and the findings of science contradict each other, I'll lay all my money on the instincts of a woman any day. I frequently use the quote about my wife from Muppet Treasure Island: *How does she bloody know?* Experience has taught me I have a greater chance of hiding something from God than I do my wife.

I don't know what Fraulein Hildegard noticed first, me bawling like a newly branded calf or bleeding like a stuck hog, but she began barking at me in Gestapo-like cadence something about *I saw what you did you little sickness and you had it coming and if I was her I'd hit you again.* The site of blood stirred up memories for the Fraulein of past tortures; she was reliving former days of gore.

I made the trip the next day to the principal's office with sulking shoulders and head bowed in shame. News of a girl bloodying a boy's nose traveled fast even before social media so as I trudged to the office, the girls looked at me in disdain and the boys patted me knowingly on the back.

I sat down in the chair across the desk from the principal with the familiar wood paddle nicknamed *The Enforcer* hanging on the wall behind his desk. That two-foot long tool of torture was administered after we were told to bend over and grab our ankles. Later, I would watch between my legs as my chubby fifth grade teacher would aim first then swing so hard her feet would come off the floor. They all learned from the bus drivers how to administer the most amount of pain with the least amount of effort.

"So," he growled. "I hear you tried to kiss Candace? Is that true?"

"Yes, *Mein Fuhrer,* I mean, Mr. Jones." I mumbled

"You know you're not supposed to do things like that, right?"

"Yes, Mr. Jones, but I guess I'm a bit confused." I admitted, "I was in here recently for the Pippi Longstocking incident after she jumped me from the merry-go-round so I just thought that all girls want to be kissed. Help me understand: what do girls really want?"

I discovered a topic upon which Mr. Jones could wax eloquent: the complexity of the female species. He pontificated for what seemed like hours about the mysterious delights and devices of women. Even though I was still only in second grade, I surmised he didn't understand them any better than I did. *The Enforcer* hung silently on the wall.

As he stood up to walk me out of the office he put his fatherly hand on my shoulder and asked, "So have you learned your lesson?"

"Yes, Mr. Jones, no man really knows the mind of a woman."

"Correct. And if you ever figure that out, son, you can have my job." Mr. Jones softened. "But trust me, they want chocolates and roses first before you ever try something like that again."

Why Little Boys Should Never Practice Medicine

L ittle kids should never be left alone to practice medicine on themselves, their friends, or their pets. They tend to ignore the *do no harm* part of the Hippocratic Oath. Most of the treatments they prescribe are based on witchcraft and voodoo rather than science.

A case in point.

I grew up in the country so I always wanted to be a cowboy and everybody knows that cowboys don't run around barefoot. Cowboys, after all, die with their boots on. The only people I knew that ran around barefoot were long-haired-hippie-freaks and my nephew from New York, Jeff Miller. Although Jeff was not a hippie, he lived close enough to Woodstock to be influenced by osmosis.

Hillbillies are known to run around barefoot, but country kids

61

from Kansas are not. The reasons we didn't were largely because of two things: animal dung and sand burrs. One does not want to step barefoot in a freshly minted cow-pie while racing from The Cows of Hobson's Pond. Stephen King has yet to write a horror novel that will make you convulse quite like stepping barefoot in a fresh cow-pie.

The other enemy of barefootin' are sand burrs, little Torture Devices from Hell. About the size of a pea, they spread out on the ground so you don't just step on one at a time, you step on forty-six at a time. They are as mean as middle school cheerleaders.

I tried once to run around barefoot, but never could get the hang of it. To this day, if I walk barefoot across a graveled road I dance like a hillbilly at a hootenanny and squeal like a greased pig being chased by a bunch of little kids.

Jeff, on the other hand, could walk barefoot across molten lava. When Jeff popped out of his Momma's womb, the first thing the doctor noticed was that the bottoms of his feet were made of leather:

"Mrs. Miller," the doctor said. "The soles of your new baby's feet are made out of leather."

"I'm not surprised," my sister, Carmen, said. "The way he's been kicking the last four months I swear he was wearing cowboy boots and spurs."

"At least you won't waste a lot of money buying shoes for him."

"Just as long as he doesn't grow up to be a hippie, I'll be okay. But I was kind of hoping for cowboy. I kind of like cowboys."

One summer Jeff convinced me that I needed to go barefoot. He was a year older than me and I held him in the highest esteem, even to the point of hero worship. I worked hard to hear him say, "Well done, thou good and faithful servant."

However, my Mom saw my lemming-like inclination with Jeff and often questioned my logic.

"Would you jump off a cliff if he told you to?"

"Yes, Mother, I would," I dutifully responded.

One hot summer day we were racing through yard and I cut the underside of my big toe on a piece of glass. I looked down to see a gusher of blood erupting from my foot. I howled like a coyote caught in a steel trap. As I writhed in pain, Jeff grabbed his EMS gear and began performing triage.

"We need to get inside, quick, before you die," he said as he put his stethoscope away.

"But I don't want to die," I wailed. "I'm only nine-years-old."

Jeff reaffirmed my growing concerns about my imminent demise when he asked if he could have my Hot Wheels collection. I hopped inside with one hand on his shoulder and the other hand tightly squeezing the gaping wound. Copious amounts of blood spilled on the linoleum as I sat down on the kitchen chair. Jeff quickly handed me a wet dishrag to stop the bleeding.

"I think that might need stitches," he offered.

I had three great fears in my childhood: missing the rapture, my niece, Colleen Miller, and the hospital. I saw the inside of a hospital once when my Dad was recuperating from surgery. He opened his robe to reveal several copper staples holding together an incision from his neck to his waist. After that experience, I assumed the doctors opened you up like that every time you went to the hospital even if it was for a tonsillectomy.

In retrospect, I have a few questions about that day I was wounded. One, why was Jeff performing triage? Usually, when we were injured we immediately ran to our mothers and let them nurse us back to health. Therefore, I can only conclude that The Generals, our mothers, were off somewhere else and left us at home alone.

That leads to my second question: Who, in their right minds, ever thought it was a good idea to leave us home alone?

"Let me look at it again," Jeff said. "I might be able to help."

I pulled back the dishrag and started bleeding like a stuck hog again. I wailed louder.

"I know just what you need. This works every time." Jeff jumped up and ran to the kitchen cabinets.

Since Jeff was all that stood between life and death for me, my spirit soared with confidence in his ability to keep me alive just a little bit longer. Reaching into the kitchen cabinet, he pulled out the blue, round carton marked, "Morton Salt."

"Are you sure about this?" I whimpered.

"Yes," Jeff confidently said. "I use it all the time to seal up deep cuts. Works like a charm."

"But won't it hurt?" I trembled somewhere in that chasm between absolute terror and wilting hope.

"Nope, not one bit."

"Should we pray first?"

"Probably wouldn't hurt."

"Dear Lord, thank you for this day and the food we're about, oh, wait, wrong prayer, I mean thank you for the miracle of modern medicine and for Jeff. Please be with the missionaries in Africa and forgive the people who decided it was a good idea to leave the two of us at home alone today. Amen."

Jeff launched into a scientific explanation about how large amounts of salt poured in an open wound provide instant coagulation of blood, numb the surrounding nerves, and heal the wound almost immediately so we could run back outside and torment the cows again.

Jeff was much more scientific than I was. One often found him peering through a microscope at the things he grew in petri dishes in his bedroom and found under the basement stairs. He could wax long and eloquent on the nature of scientific rationale and I sat mesmerized as he talked, thus elevating his hero status in my heart. Salt was obviously the cure for all that ailed the human race.

Again, I have to ask: Who thought it was a good idea to leave us alone?

Trust me, he said, *I do this all the time*, he said, *it won't hurt a bit*, he said.

I opened the wound and he poured in the salt.

After Mom arrived home, several neighbors called and asked her why the ambulance was at our house. Mom reassured them that no ambulance had been there that day and wasn't sure what they were talking about. Apparently, about three o'clock in the afternoon, most of the neighbors within a two-mile range heard what sounded like an ambulance wailing.

Mom launched a full-scale investigation after she hung up from the last phone call. She saw the bloody dishrag in the trash; saw bloody fingerprints on the Morton Salt container; saw bloody footprints on the kitchen ceiling; saw the curtains ripped to shreds; saw all the crystal shattered in the china cabinet; saw the dog whimpering in the corner like it was shell-shocked; saw the cat having a seizure on the floor and saw that the milk in the fridge turned to cottage cheese. She then hauled me into the dimly lit interrogation room.

"What happened?" she began.

"I cut my foot on piece of glass," I replied.

"Why were you barefoot? I thought you wanted to be a cowboy and everybody knows that cowboys don't run around barefoot."

"I know. It's just that Jeff said that I was a sissy if I didn't run around barefoot and I don't want to be a sissy."

"So would you jump off a cliff if he told you to?"

"Yes, Mother," I replied dutifully. "I would."

"So where did all the noise come from the neighbors called about?" She kept grilling me.

"It may or may not have been me screaming after we poured salt in my cut."

"You did *what?* Why did you pour, oh, good grief, never mind, Jeff told you to, right?"

"Yes, Mother, he did." I sat proudly.

Mom mumbled something about *us being the death of her* and *The Cows of Hobson's Pond were right about little boys being stoopid* and *who in their right mind thought it was a good idea to leave these two little idiots at home alone for the afternoon.*

Jeff found more important research to conduct while I was being interrogated and later checked in on me while doing his rounds. He was pleased I held up so well under cross-examination and that I now held scientific discovery in such high esteem. He patted me on the head and said, "Well done, thou good and faithful servant."

For a splendid moment in time, heaven came down and glory filled my soul.

Getting Our Mouths Washed Out with Soap

I prefer the taste of a bar of Dove soap compared to Zest or Dial. I ought to know, I had my mouth washed out with a variety of brands through the years. There were two reasons the soap bar got lathered up for a good scrubbing of my mouth: Sassing and Cussing. Apparently the soap was supposed to clean words *after* they came out of my mouth. My problem was that I had opinions that I thought should matter.

The surest way to have one's head removed from one's body was to sass my Mother. Had she lived during the Wild West, she would have been the fastest gunslinger north of the Pecos. If I sassed her and happened to be within arms reach, I never saw her gun clear the leather. She'd whip her hand out of the holster, cock the hammer, pull the trigger and unload all six shells in the chamber while I was still eating my peas.

Also known as *talking back,* sassing was the eighth Deadly

Sin. There are supposed to only be seven Deadly Sins, but we were good Protestants and had close to a hundred. Along with greed, lust, and pride, sassing an adult slathered one's slippery slide into hell with bear grease. Yes, Ma'am. No, sir. Yes, sir. These were the only correct answers to anything an adult said.

One incident that comes to my mind was also the same incident in which my Mom introduced me to the conundrum of global hunger. We were sitting at the dinner table in that drafty old two-story house along Highway 54 when she dropped a glob of spinach on my plate. It looked, and smelled, like someone upchucked.

I couldn't even get my dog to eat it and I had seen that cur eat the vilest of carrion. He routinely dragged rotting carcasses into the yard like they were gold medals he won at the Canine Olympics. He'd carry those things around grinning like Jimmy Carter on the campaign trail and offer me the spoils of his discovery. He took great offense if I did not share his enthusiasm for maggot-covered possum. But canned spinach? Nope, he covered his eyes with his paws and started dry heaving.

Mom put her hands on her hips and said, "Well, you know, there are starving children in Africa who would love to have that food." Thusly, I learned the most common messaging of about global hunger that persists to this day: *It's a big problem. It's somewhere Over There. You should feel bad about it. There's not a darn thing you can do about it except hand out food.*

While she was standing there glaring at me, I got out the bear grease and slathered up my own slide. What coiled her up most was me asking for the names and address of the children so I could mail the spinach to them.

Seeing her reaction, I quickly offered to eat the entire bar of soap as long as I didn't have to touch the spinach. Apparently, the loathing of spinach is genetic because years later, my young son, Caleb, insisted he eat spinach so he could be like Popeye. After his first bite he began wailing, "Ewww, gross, it's sliding down my throat."

The other reason we got our mouth washed out was for cussing, a perennial pick in the Top-Ten List of Deadly Sins.

One incident occurred during Fix It Yourself (F.I.Y.) night. Mom was a great cook, but she went on strike each Sunday afternoon and turned Sunday evenings into F.I.Y. night. Dad and we kids were left to our own defenses to scavenge for food. The dog always offered to help, but we politely refused. To make matters worse, since Dad was a minister he invited someone to lunch on Sunday after church so there were seldom any leftovers. All of us kids agreed it was a crying shame.

My nephew, Kendall, and my niece, Annie, spent a great portion of their life in our house so each Sunday night we surrendered our tummies to the culinary gods like Chef Boyardee and the Jolly Green Giant. Our favorite delicacy was the Chef's pizza that came in a little box. We'd mix the dough, spread it out on a cookie sheet, smother it with the Chef's special sauce, and fifteen minutes later have a delectable, savory delight followed two hours later by stomach cramps.

The three of us were busy cooking away one Sunday evening when Kendall- who was two years younger than me- started mocking me. I hate being mocked. So I dug out the bear grease, slathered up my slide so I could go to hell a bit faster, and called him a *little bastard*.

Mom rounded the corner to the kitchen when that dirty little word shot out of my mouth; her timing was impeccable. She always managed to show up at that optimal time to catch me with the maximum amount of guilt. Always. She showed up when I was returning the punch that Kendall threw first; she showed up when I was redressing the Barbie doll that Annie just handed me; she showed up while I was shaving a stripe down the middle of my head at the dog's suggestion; she always showed up when it looked like I was as guilty as, well, sin. Always.

"What did you call him?" she barked.

I wasn't good at thinking quickly on my feet, so I just stood there like a mute bank robber holding bags of cash in each hand with a cop pointing a gun at me.

"Figurine," Kendall replied, "he called me a figurine."

There are moments in time when reason will just get up, leave the room and slam the door behind itself and leave everyone with their mouths agape in befuddlement. Watch C-Span if you don't believe me.

On one hand, I appreciated Kendall's valor and intent. Our typical *modus operandi* was to shove each other in front of oncoming trains with reckless abandon and little remorse. However, in this instance Kendall was to be commended for attempting to rescue a fallen comrade. *Trying* is sometimes as important as *triumph.*

On the other hand, the synapses in the frontal lobe of my brain were exploding like someone just threw a firecracker in a shed full of dynamite. My powers of reason were trying to make sense out of the situation and to answer the pressing question: Why did he think *figurine* sounded like *bastard*?

The conversation in the Command Center for Logic in the frontal lobe of my brain went like this:

Commander: "Soldier, give me your report. Do the words start with the same letter?"

Soldier: "No, sir. One start with F, the other starts with B."

Commander: "Do they have the same number of syllables?"

Soldier: "No, sir. One has two syllables, the other has three."

Commander: "How many letters do they share?"

70

Soldier: "Just one, sir, the letter 'r'."

Commander: "Do they rhyme?"

Soldier: "No, sir. Not even close."

Commander: "Very well. Abort mission. Send all reports to Area 51."

There's nothing like obfuscation to interrupt the normal flow of reason. Politicians do this all the time. Why would it not work for dumb little country kids like us?

I expected a trip to the sink and having my Chef Boyardee replaced with a good scrubbing of Dove. Instead, Mom backed away slowly, kind of like a person sneaking away from a mess they've made and don't want to hang around and clean it up. I heard her mutter something about *that made no sense whatsoever* and *they can slather all the bear grease they want on their slides* and *who in their right mind thought it was a good idea to leave those little idiots alone in the kitchen..*

Kendall, Annie, and I resumed our fine dining experience. We compared notes and debriefed each other on the recent encounter with Mom. Few conclusions were drawn that were substantive in nature, but since Kendall spared me the gallows, we toasted the hero with enthusiastic *huzzahs* and sang several rounds of *for he's a jolly good fellow*. Even the dog joined in.

Years later, after the statute of limitations expired, we regaled Dad with the *figurine* story around a dinner table. Dad recalled a very similar situation when he was a young boy and called his brother, Bill, a bastard. However, Bill came to the rescue when Dad was put in front of the firing squad and cried, "He called me *Baxter*, not *bastard*." Now that is logic I can get behind.

The three of us kids learned a very valuable lesson that seems to serve Congress very well: If you can't dazzle them with logic, bewilder them with absurdity.

Learning to Smoke and Chew

If the Marlboro Man were to be believed, smoking a cigarette would put hair on my twelve-year-old chest and help me ride a horse like a real cowboy. Or I could put a pinch of Skoal between my cheek and gum like Larry Mahan, the Rodeo Champ, and ride bulls with the best of them. These things are important to a little boy growing up in Kansas.

However, I lived with Puritans who put Smoking and Chewing on the list of Top Ten Deadly sins that were unacceptable in our little country church. They were just another way for a person to slather an extra layer of bear grease on that slippery slide into hell. Although Gossiping and Judging Others were on that list and practiced to perfection, they were far more acceptable than Smoking or Chewing.

In addition to memorizing Bible verses to make sure we

walked the straight-and-narrow, we also memorized the sing-songy incantation: *I don't smoke and I don't chew and I don't run around with girls that do.*

For all of Dad's knowledge about the Holy Scripture, he never quite figured out that humans have a tendency not to follow rules someone else makes up. Instead, humans prefer to make up their own rules and then not follow them. He told us not to smoke or chew so, of course, we wanted to. If it was a sin, it must be fun.

The whole rule-making thing started off in the Garden of Eden and, well, we all know how that ended. There are three very important lessons that human beings learned in the conversation between God and Adam in the Garden: deny, make counter-accusations, and play the role of a victim.

If it worked for Adam, then why wouldn't it work for the rest of us, especially Congress? I imagine the conversation in the Garden went like this:

God: Why are you hiding?

Adam: We're not; we're looking for our clothes.

God: Who said you needed clothes?

Adam: Eve did. I got out of the shower and did a little *woo-woo-woo* and she told me to put some clothes on.

God: Did you eat the fruit?

Adam: No, Eve did. I just nibbled.

God: You had one rule. Just one; you only had one rule.

Adam: Eve made me do it.

Eve: The devil made me do it.

Adam: Would you please punish Eve for making fun of me?

Thus began the human race's relationship with rules.

Naturally, we did what we were told not to do. We needed to experiment with Smoking and Chewing. However, our biggest problem was access to contraband. My nephew, Kendall, and I wanted to try both smoking AND chewing, but there wasn't a Kwik Mart near so we could con a homeless person into buying us some tobacco. Therefore, we had no choice but to resort to crime; we stole it from my older brothers.

It should be noted that it wasn't really that bad a crime since we didn't steal what we wanted: cigarettes. Instead, we stole the only thing they had: a pipe and Borkum Riff tobacco.

It should also be noted that a pipe is not the handiest thing to start a smoking career because those darn things are nearly impossible to keep lit, especially when you're hiding under the bed of a old pickup truck. I don't know why we thought hiding under that old truck was a good idea. I suppose in our little idiot minds we thought if Mom or Dad looked out into the pasture and saw smoke coming out from under that dilapidated truck, they would assume the packrats were making s'mores over a campfire. No one ever accused of us being brain surgeons.

We hid the pipe and tobacco behind the seat of the truck inside the packrat nest and one day, while Kendall was gone, I decided to smoke solo. I sucked on that pipe trying to get the pipe lit and, in frustration, finally piled a bunch of tobacco on the ground and lit it on fire. I never actually smoked, but I smelled like I'd slid down a chimney when I walked into the house.

Dad: What were you doing out by that old truck?

Me: Um, looking for my clothes.

Dad: Were you smoking?

Me: Um.

The Cows of Hobson's Pond

Where was Kendall when I needed him? After he substituted figurine for bastard, surely he could come up with some obfuscation now.

Me: I was burning something.

Dad: What were you burning?

Me: Bear grease.

As I said, no one ever thought I had a future as a brain surgeon.

I learned to put up with Mom and the Generals being mad at me, but I was mortified at the thought of Dad, the Commander-in-Chief, being mad at me. As Jeff often said, Mom and the Generals were like BB guns pelting you as you canoed down the river, but Dad was a Howitzer that blew everything to smithereens when it went off, which, thankfully was rare.

Surprisingly, Joe, the visiting evangelist, rescued me from the firing squad. If you read the story about the evangelist and his marimba-playing wife, you know visiting evangelists ranked somewhere in my least-favorite things between a bath each night and liver and onions.

Joe: "I got off the city bus in Chicago the other day and the first thing my wife said to me was that I smelled like I was a smoker. This boy must have been around something like that."

It turns out the spirit of Kendall was alive and well. What Joe said made no sense to anyone since I had never even seen a city bus in my country-boy life. But I nodded in agreement with Joe.

It was Dad's turn to walk away muttering something about *that made no sense whatsoever* and *he can slather all the bear grease he wants on his slide* and *who in their right mind thought it was a good idea to leave that little idiot alone in the pasture.*

Later that year, during the winter, we had the good fortune of

76

having a fellow derelict, Rod Busby, show up to play a bit of ice hockey on Hobson's Pond. The first freeze of the pond coincided with a Northerner raging out of the artic circle so the ice froze with ridges like a washboard. It was awful to skate on, but it was all we had. The cows apparently flew south each winter with the geese so they weren't there to make snide remarks about our hockey skills. In addition, the cows would have volunteered to be cheerleaders and the Good Lord knows they look awful in skirts. I'm sure one of them would have wanted to officiate and the only thing worse that a bovine fan at a hockey game is a bovine referee.

Rod had older brothers, too, but they didn't smoke; they chewed tobacco. Glory, hallelujah! We had us some Red Man big leaf chew.

It was in second grade in Mrs. Beulah Bohn's class that I first witnessed the chain-reaction of little boys upchucking. Frank Stubblefield lost his cookies on the painted gray concrete floor and Mrs. Bohn quickly shouted, "Don't anyone look."

Naturally, we did what we were told not to do. She had never learned that lesson either about someone else making up rules because we all looked and, sure enough, three-quarters of the class lost their school lunch that today including yours, truly.

Our first hint that trouble was brewing on Hobson's Pond was when Rod opened that Red Man pouch and told us all to take a deep breath through our nostrils so as to savor the flavor. It was at that precise moment the volcano in our tummies started moving on the Richter scale. We stuffed a wad in our cheeks and started playing hockey.

It was somewhere between the first and second period we discovered that laying down naked on the ice while dry heaving was the only thing that alleviated the misery.

Global warming hadn't kicked in yet so our beloved Hobson's Pond stayed frozen and was stained with little blotches for the rest of the winter. There were also indentations in the ice shaped like a human body curled up in fetal positions. Some little rat told the cows when they returned in the spring so we had to listen to them all summer make fun of us while they chased us through the pasture.

I swore off any tobacco products until my later teen years when I, once again, thought it was cool to smoke. I started smoking when I was eighteen to prove I was a man and three years later tried to quit to prove the same thing.

These are just a few of the reasons I never grew up to be a brain surgeon.

Meet the Elmer Fudd of Hunters

I didn't mean to shoot Mom in the leg with my Red Ryder BB gun. But by the time she realized I was the little idiot that raised a pea-sized welt on her leg, I made it into the protective circle of the Cows of Hobson's Pond. It was the first, and only, time they came to my rescue. They witnessed it all and testified that it was a complete accident. I had to promise them alfalfa pellets and listen to them chant at me, *Hey Elmer Fudd, kill the Wabbit, kill the Wabbit.*

We lived in the country so naturally we had a variety of rifles, shotguns, pistols and BB guns. Contemporary reasoning assumes I should have grown up to be a serial killer with all those guns around.

Since my Dad had his *you kill it, you eat it* rule, I never was much of a hunter. Therefore, I often shot at things that didn't have to be gutted, plucked, or skinned. One Christmas, I broke his rule about *you sneak a peek at your presents and you'll lose them.* I found the Red Ryder hidden in the closet and it was the first time I ever uttered the word *sexy.* Give me a BB gun and a few tin cans and, to this day, I can whittle away an afternoon with pure delight. We call that *plinkin'.*

Dad had a few rules about guns: always assume they're loaded; never point them at anyone, always check the barrel to make sure it's not plugged because Kendall stuck it in the mud while you were hunting ducks; clean it when you're done; if you kill it, you eat it; Don't shoot anyone, especially family; and a gun is never responsible for a crime, the idiot holding the gun is responsible for the crime.

One summer evening I donned my Fudd-like cap and went plinkin'. Plinkin' was a lot more fun than hunting because hunting usually involved walking long distances in grass taller than me. I was so skittish from being chased by the Cows of Hobson's Pond that scaring up a covey of quail short-circuited all the electrical impulses to my heart.

Doctors insist you spend thousands of dollars for stress tests to check your heart, but I can save you a lot of money by walking you thru a covey of quail. Quail wait for you to walk over the top of them then fly up your boxers. If you're still alive after flushing six coveys of quail, then your heart has at least another hundred thousand miles on it.

But plinkin' tin cans got boring so I looked for other things to shoot. Now, remember, I didn't grow up with iPads, or Nintendos so my level of entertainment might seem, well, like a redneck, but you make the best with what ya' got to work with.

I found a dead locust lying on the ground and decided it might be fun to shoot. Since it was already dead when I found it, Dad might not make me skin and eat it. So I laid it on a big rock in our yard to plink.

Dad dragged home huge round rocks that looked like sixteen-inch tall biscuits with hundreds of perforated holes. He then painted them white and they served as nice decorations spotted on our one acre yard.

The biscuit rocks were also the perfect height as footstools for metal lawn chairs with curved legs that made them like rocker-recliners. Mom decided to enjoy the summer evening reading a book while rocking gently in one of those metal chairs. She was wearing a duster - a loose fitting cottony gown- and propped her bare legs up on the rock.

Crime Scene Investigators (CSI) would later reconstruct the scene. Numerous laws of nature were broken in order for me to shoot Mom in the leg since she was sitting at a 90-degree angle to the left of where I aimed. Apparently the head of the locust is made of Kevlar.

Dad heard the scream and thought that Mom had been baptized by the Holy Ghost and turned into a Charismatic; either that or demons got a hold of her. Either one was a valid explanation to her histrionics and carried with it the equal amount of shame to this way of thinking. What led him to believe the latter explanation was her frantically chasing me across the yard screaming something about, *who in their right mind left Elmer Fudd alone with a gun.*

The other time I shot at something that was already dead makes perfect sense after you give me a chance to explain it.

North of our house about thirty miles was Cassoday, Kansas: The Prairie Chicken Capital of the World. During the '60's and '70's, Cassoday was a destination for chicken hunters.

The only experience I had shooting a chicken was Ralph, our nasty old rooster that attacked little children and old ladies wearing dusters. My Red Ryder didn't have enough power to kill him or even knock him out, but man-oh-man, I could rile him with a shot to the body. Ralph and Mom shared the same reaction to getting shot: jump three feet off the ground then start chasing me.

However, prairie chickens are not as easy to shoot. They are the Usain Bolts of the aviary kingdom and can ratchet it up to 35 miles per hour. Ralph could match their speed when Mom chased him with a two-by-four. I offered her my gun for those expeditions, but she mumbled something about not wanting to be an Elmer Fudd herself and have the sheriff haul her away for shooting me.

My older brothers planned for weeks in anticipation of the opening morning of prairie chicken season. They oiled their stocks; I oiled mine. They cleaned their barrels; I cleaned mine. They checked their ammo; I checked mine. They packed their lunch; I packed mine. They went to Cassoday to hunt; I went to Rosalia to help Dad remodel a house. *He is too little,* they said; *he will be in the way,* they said; *he will start whining,* they said, *he shoots like Elmer Fudd,* they said.

Dad later explained that the real reason he sided with them had more to do with me being thrown in a pit and sold to a passing band of Egyptians than it did with any of their logic.

I had aged enough to carry a rifle so I conned Dad into letting me hunt in the pasture outside of his rental house. I wandered up a ravine expecting a covey quail to fly up my boxers when I spotted a prairie chicken under a thicket. I froze, expecting him to lurch like Mom launching out of that old rocker, but he never moved. I inched closer: no movement. Closer: nothing. I finally poked him with a stick. He was dead.

I dragged him out from under the thicket to discover he was still warm. I surmised that he had been hit with a shotgun pellet up north and made it this far before resting in peace.

Well, okay, he didn't exactly rest in peace because I wouldn't let him. My thought process went something like this:

- I had brothers who left me behind and I wanted revenge
- I had a dead, but still very warm bird in my hand
- The bird showed no sign of being injured, even though it was dead

- I could make it look like I had taken it fair and square

So I shot it in the head and took it back to Dad.

Dad: Where did you find that bird, Elmer?

Me: I shot it on the fly.

Dad: You shot a prairie chicken on the fly? The last time you shot something I had to talk your Mom out of sending you to the orphanage.

Me: Yep, it was taking off and I pulled the gun up and shot it. See, the head has a bullet hole in it.

How could he argue with me? I didn't fess up until the statute of limitations expired and I had kids of my own.

We ate roasted prairie chicken for dinner that night. Rather, I should say *some of us* ate *one* roasted prairie chicken for dinner that night. My brothers wasted four boxes of shells and missed every bird and would not touch mine. It appeared I dropped my bird with one bullet. They seethed and threatened to look for a roving band of Egyptians.

After the dishes were done, I heard Mom and Dad talking:

Dad: Did that bird taste okay to you?

Mom: I thought it was quite tasty but I did find some buckshot in it.

Dad: Yeah, me too. I think I chipped my dentures. Think we ought to tell the boys what really happened?

Mom: Nope, if we do that, little Elmer Fudd's liable to shoot me again.

It's been a lot of years since then, but I keep a Red Ryder by my back door at all times. I still think it's pretty sexy.

The Tent that Almost Killed Me

The first tent I owned darn near ruined me for camping. I'm not complaining that it was too big, but it required two elephants and a dozen Amish barn builders to erect. It wasn't like a pup tent that weighs 3 ounces and pops into shape when you throw it on the ground. No-sir-eee-bob, ours could hold a battalion of Marines. My sister's Boyfriend thought he could win us kids over by giving us an old army tent and he was right; everyone has a price and ours was a tent.

The tent was big; it was green; it was ours; and it almost killed us. However, the Boyfriend's status diminished considerably each time we went camping.

I was taught never to look a gift horse in the mouth so I won't start whinin'. In my Dad's estimation, Whinin' was right behind Cussing and Sassing in his Top Ten List of Deadly Sins. So I'm not *whinin'*, I'm just *sayin'* that a ten-year-old boy's first tent ought to be one he can put up with the help of a dog. But all I had was my younger nephew Kendall who disappeared at the first hint of manual labor. Always.

Furthermore, the tent should be light enough a little boy can go camping on the spur of the moment instead of having to hit the weight room and steroids for two months in advance.

There are a number of problems for a ten-year-old camping in Kansas with a tent the size of a Winnebago. One problem was that the tent, like us, wasn't all there. Three of the stakes, one of the poles, and six of the tie-downs were missing.

Another problem was the wind. Kansas was named after the Native American tribe, Kansa, which, roughly translated means *south-wind-that-blows-harder-than-Brian-Williams-on-the-six-o'clock-news.*

We don't find our true north in Kansas by looking for a star or seeing what side of the tree the moss grows on. Instead, we look at which direction the trees lean; they all lean to the north since the wind predominantly blows out of the south. My sister, Carmen, once took a sapling home to New York where the wind never blew and, sure enough, the tree leaned to the north.

An additional problem for little boys camping in Kansas was coyotes. Just to be clear, they are pronounced *kuy-yotes,* not *kuy-yo-tees.* When coyotes start howling, well, little boys have been known to wet themselves in broad daylight. Coyotes are attracted to high-pitched screams, like those of a dying rabbit. It turns out that dying rabbits and ready-to-wet-themselves ten-year-old boys emit the same sounds.

For us, the prime camping ground was the shores of Hobson's Pond. However, there was one significant challenge: The Cows of Hobson's Pond. It took a lot of courage to set up the tent because we knew the ridicule we would suffer at the hand of the cows. Cows were like our mothers, the Generals, who had an opinion about every little thing we kids thought, said, did, or wanted to do.

We tried camping on Hobson's Pond once, but they stood outside our tent all night long, mooing. Cows are like college kids; they'll pull an all-nighter if they think there's fun to be had.

Maude, the cow, whispered after it got dark, "Hey, hey little kids. The boogey-man is coming to get you."

"My Mom said there's no such thing as a boogey-man," I wailed.

"Oh, yeah? Well, we see them hanging around outside your bedroom window all the time. And if the boogeyman doesn't get you, the coyotes will."

"I have a gun!" I quivered.

"Oh, is this the same Red Ryder you shot your Mom with? We stood up for you once, buckwheat, but you're camping in our house now."

"I'm not afraid!" I shouted through the tent wall.

"Did you know Charles Manson broke out of prison and he's coming this way? He's riding with the Hell's Angels, too. They like torturing little boys. And Walter Cronkite said the Russians are going to nuke us tonight. Besides that, the Rapture happened twenty-minutes ago and your Mom and Dad made it, but you didn't. You've been Left Behind! We're calling Truman Capote, too. He'll like this story."

Conversations like this are the reason The Cows of Hobson's Pond are responsible for my neurosis.

We lasted 'till about midnight then decided that the quarter-mile run home dodging cow pies in the dark was better than the increasing terror the cows were inflicting on us.

Next time, we decided to camp closer to home in our yard under the big cottonwood tree. We called the Amish, hitched the elephants, and set the tent up. The Amish volunteered to bring their families of ten kids each and spend the night with us since there was plenty of room, but we took a rain check.

Dad: "You boys know there is a storm coming tonight?"

Me: "Yep, but we're not afraid."

Dad: "Okay, we'll leave the light on for you just in case."

The tent had no floor, so we threw our sleeping bags on the grass and cuddled up with the chiggers for the night. When I think of my childhood, my first thought is often of chiggers. Once they came out during the spring, I was covered with chigger bites until the first frost. The only relief I got was to fire up Dad's belt sander and remove my first layer of skin. I spent my childhood looking like I had a perpetual case of the measles or the Russians had finally nuked us.

Kendall and I told a few ghost stories, agreed that this was more pleasant than the night with the Cows, and vowed that we were staying in the tent even if a tornado came. We then drifted off to dream of hunting bears with Daniel Boone.

Daniel's musket exploded at the same time the first clap of thunder levitated our little bodies above the bed of chiggers. The pelting rain and wind slammed against the side of our tent like our Moms yelling at us to quit playing in the street. Soon, water started running in on the bare ground but, by golly, after Mom made fun of us for coming home early from Hobson's Pond, we weren't about to go inside.

The tent flapped the way Dad described one of the Lollipops (Little Old Ladies of the Party Line Society); *her tongue is hinged in the middle and flaps on both ends.*

We moved closer to the middle but the groundwater found us and started us on the journey to Hypothermia-ville. However, we were so determined to ride out the storm that only the Rapture could have dislodged us from that tent. Never have two young souls more earnestly prayed for the return of Jesus.

88

The pelting rain turned into large dump trucks unloading entire lakes of water on us. The tent might have stayed upright if all of the parts were accounted for, but they were not and it did not. It collapsed around our shivering little bodies like a wet towel the size of Texas covers two drowned mice. My gosh it was heavy.

Coyotes usually stay in their dens during a storm, but the sound of dying rabbits above the clamor was too much to resist. It seemed like no matter which way Kendall and I crawled, the sound of them howling moved in front of us.

Mom was waiting for us when we finally stumbled inside just before the coyotes ate us. She had big, dry towels and was muttering something about *who in their right mind thought it was a good idea to let these little idiots set up a tent with a storm coming* and *I wonder what happened to those dying little rabbits outside?*

Dad handed out medals for bravery and said that discretion is the better part of valor. The next day, he took the tent to the Army surplus store to trade for a smaller one.

The owner recognized it. "Yeah, some guy came in here a while back and traded me out of that tent. He said he was going to use it to bribe some idiot kids of a chick he was dating. I told him it was not quite all there and he said *that's okay, the kids aren't either so it should work just fine.*"

Dad got a smaller version we could handle without the Amish.

We never saw that Boyfriend again.

The Night I Walked on Water

L ike Jesus, I once walked on water. His reason was much nobler than mine since it was all about faith. Mine was based on pure, unadulterated terror; it was all about fear.

I never understood why monsters only come out at night. I could reach under my bed anytime during the day to retrieve toys, the cat, or the lizard the cat was after, but let the nightfall and not even Jesus could get my leg over the side of the bed.

My older siblings routinely ignored the warnings not to tease me about monsters hiding under my bed. *Hey Rick, if your leg touches the floor at night the monster will drag you under and we'll never see you again.* This, apparently, is hereditary because, once I had sons, I heard them do the same thing to each other.

The scariest movie I ever saw was the Wizard of Oz until I

went to New York to visit Jeff and his family. If you live in Kansas, then Oz is part of your DNA. Along with learning how to write in cursive, we were taught all the lines and to cackle wicked-witch-of-the-east-like, *I'll get you my pretty.*

There is a striking parallel between the movie and my real life. Mine, too, is the story of an innocent young child in Kansas being tormented by a wicked witch from the east. And where did my niece Colleen live? East of Kansas in New York.

The Wizard of Oz helped me much later in life to converse with people when they discover I'm from Kansas.

Stranger at a party: "You're from Kansas? Do you have a pair of red slippers?"

Me: "Nope. I gave up cross dressing when I broke my ankle."

Stranger: "How's Dorothy and Toto?"

Me: "Dorothy's in a nursing home and they stuffed Toto and put him in the Smithsonian."

Stranger: "How's the lion, the tin man, and the guy made of straw?"

Me: "Fine. They're all in Congress now."

My first mistake was letting Jeff keep me up one night to watch a horror flick, *The Skull.* I sat with my ten-year-old feet drawn up in a fetal position for two hours of pure black and white panic. Jeff was accustomed to this kind of terror since he lived with Colleen and they giggled through it like it was Gilligan's Island.

The worst part was when it ended and I had to go sleep with Jeff in his big bed in the basement where monsters hid under the stairs and ate little children. Jeff said there were numerous stories in the Red Hook Gazette about them.

After my heart slowed to the rhythm of a rabbit thumping on three shots of espresso, I finally drifted off to sleep. That was my second mistake. Jeff decided to crawl down to the end of the bed and clamp both hands on to the calf of my leg.

After my tent almost killed me in the middle of the night, you would have thought my parents were accustomed to the sound of a dying rabbit. That was not the case; Mom stood at the head of the stairs and growled out something about *"who in their right might thought it was a good idea to let that little idiot watch a scary movie* and *you'd think by now I could tell the sound between a dying rabbit and Rick squealing like a stuck-hog.* She didn't want to go down the stairs either.

Although most of the monsters I encountered were imaginary, I did, however, meet a real, live, *I'm-going-to-eat-you-and-all-your-babies* monster the next summer when Jeff came back to Kansas.

Jeff had a crusty old bald-headed uncle that was a legendary fisherman in our parts, Max Graves. Any bait shop within a hundred miles had a Polaroid of Max holding a behemoth flathead catfish that was large enough to eat three small children at a time.

Jeff asked me one night if I wanted to run bank lines with Max on the Walnut River. That was like being invited to climb Mount Everest with Sir Edmund Hillary.

Max was no nonsense and let me know it was a rarity for him to take little kids fishing.

"I've heard tell that you scream like a rabbit dying," Max said.

"Maybe," I replied.

"Okay, well, if you do I'll just have to use you as bait. Catfish like little kids that scream like dying rabbits and thrash around in the water."

Many of the catfish Max caught could easily eat a ten-year-old boy. I wondered if he'd hang me from a bank line or just throw in the deep part of the river on the trotline.

During the spring, the Walnut River screamed through the fields of Kansas like me running from Jeff after he clamped his hands on my leg. However, in the summer it was a lazy, muddy river that snaked through Kansas during the humid nights of July like a 500-pound person motoring around Wally World on a scooter.

We spent the late evening baiting the bank lines and trotlines with live perch. We went back to sleep for a bit, and then woke up in the middle of the night to run the lines. You'd be surprised how noisy a summer night can be on the banks of a Kansas river when all the critters come out to play. It is a veritable chorus with the crickets carrying the rhythm, the bullfrogs thumping out the base like a car-full of teenagers at a stoplight, and the coyotes howling in harmony. I occasionally sang along in high soprano when a spider dropped off a branch on to my lap.

Max climbed in the middle of the old johnboat to be the oarsman and I got on one end, Jeff in the other. A dark river without any moonlight and only a wienie flashlight with dying batteries is downright creepy. But Max had built in night vision so he navigated us from bank line to bank line and around the logjams.

After a bit, he decided to park the boat and fish. We threw our lines in and did what all catfishermen do; waited. And waited. Then we waited some more. Max finally grunted about having something on his line and it was big and he hoped it didn't break his line and you boys be ready it might be a snapping turtle.

Snapping turtles are mistakenly named; they should be clamping turtles. They have ferocious prehistoric jaws that are meant to lock on and not let go. They hiss, call you names, and dare you to stick some body part in their mouth. Ten-year-old boys are known to take them up on this dare and live to regret it. It seems the only thing that makes the turtle let go is the high-pitched sound of a dying rabbit.

Max bent his rod and lifted the snapping turtle up to the edge of the boat for us to see. That thing was the size of a truck tire and had already formed some pretty negative opinions about us. In fact, he came to the surface shouting out all kinds of turtle cusswords at us and threatened to consume the whole lot of us before the battle was over.

Max grunted a heave-ho and the growling monster landed at my feet; the snapping turtle, I mean, not Max. Mr. Snapper looked at me and assumed the hook in his mouth was my fault. He started thrashing around amidst the tackle boxes, fishing poles, and my tender little bare feet. Ten little toes wiggling in the night looked a whole lot like earthworms drowning in the river so he tried to take a few bites. My toes had finally gotten over the trauma of the *this-little-piggy-went-wee-wee-wee-all-the-way-home* game only to be traumatized by a prehistoric carnivore that thought they were hors d'oeuvres.

I knew I couldn't scream or I would become bank-line bait, but that end of the johnboat was not big enough for me and Mr. Snapper. One of us had to get out of town before sunup.

And that's when I walked on water. Or at least tried; I made it a few steps, and then sunk, just like Peter.

I never did get to go run lines with Max again. My next encounter with him at a river in the middle of the night was when he dove eighteen feet off the old stone bridge at our favorite swimming hole to show us young punks how to dive. He came up bleeding. We applauded his heroism and carved his name into the limestone.

From then, on we reverently, and affectionately, referred to him as Misguided Missile Max.

Not to his face, of course; none of us wanted to be catfish bait.

The Cows of Hobson's Pond

The One Thing That Kept Me From Running Away From Home

It was not a good sign when my Mom volunteered to pack me a lunch when I threatened to run away from home. I found a hobo stick that was longer than I was tall that would serve as a multipurpose tool of sorts. One on end, I'd wrap up all my worldly possessions in a knapsack.

On the other end, I whittled a spear-like point so I could impale any charging lion that I might encounter along the journey. I was planning on running a *long* way from home and end up hanging with the Maasai in Africa. I knew missionaries there that treated ten-year-olds far better than my Mom treated me.

I don't recall all the egregious methods of parenting my Mom was dog-piling on me, but making me eat liver-and-onions was the final straw. I had had enough; every man has his limit of enduring torture and mine was liver-and-onions.

I anticipated my announcement causing more reaction than it did. I hoped Mom would drop down on bended knee and apologize for making me eat liver-and-onions or, at the very least, drive me to Rosalia to spend the night with Kendall and Annie. She didn't even look up from ironing Dad's t-shirts while she was watching General Hospital.

Yes, she ironed my Dad's t-shirts. And underwear. It was a different era.

Me: "I'm running away from home."

Mom: "Okay."

Me: "I mean it this time. I'm leaving and never coming back."

Mom: "Want me to pack you a lunch?"

Me: "Yes, please, I'd like a bologna sandwich."

Mom: "Don't forget to wear clean underwear in case you're in an accident."

Mom could never come up with sound reasoning for why a person needed clean under wear on in case of an accident, so I went to the Oracle, my Dad.

Me: "Dad, why does a person need clean underwear on in case of an accident?"

Dad: "I'm not sure; I've never figured that out, either. When an accident happens, first you *say it* then you *do it* so the underwear end up soiled anyway. Go ask your Mom again."

Furthermore, I had a variety of fears that I kept around like pets. I'd feed and water them to make sure they stayed healthy and sometimes rescued a few from euthanasia. Occasionally, a visiting evangelist or missionary would drop off a new fear like a stray dog abandoned along our highway. It might be a picture of a nuclear warhead in Russia that was aimed at our house or a tribe of cannibals ready to boil me in beans, but I'd adopt that fear as my own. Being a good little Christian boy, those fears gave me a new way of feeling bad about not having enough faith, which ended up being a good thing after all. Feeling guilty about not having enough faith was genuine proof that I was a believer. I might make the rapture after all.

When my pet fears heard I made the decision to run away from home, they all threw a party and invited friends. They scrambled out of their cages and started jumping up and down; *Oh, boy, this sounds like fun! I wanna go! I wanna go! Pick me! Pick me!* I always had a hard time choosing teammates on the playground so I just decided to let them all go with me.

Therefore, preparation for the trip was based on what fear was the largest. Although missing the rapture was my perennial favorite of all-time-worst-fears, a different fear took center stage for my journey: *the dark*. I'd developed a nervous tic after watching *The Skull* with Jeff in New York when he took me to new levels of fear of *the dark*.

The epic journey required serious decision-making. What kind of things lurked in *the dark*? What kind of weapon would I need? Where would I find water along the way? How much food could I get in my knapsack? What if I run out of clean under wear?

I concluded that whatever was in *the dark* that posed an imminent threat could be dealt with in one of two ways: a bow-and-arrow for the long shots and a tomahawk for hand-to-hand combat. Fortunately, I had both in my arsenal.

The bow was a green fiberglass longbow about a foot taller than me. I'd collected enough nickels from the sale of pop-bottles so I bought the primitive weapon at T.G.&.Y. I purchased it to hunt on the prairie, but had yet to fine-tune my marksmanship to be a serious threat to anything other than a hay bale or the Cows of Hobson's Pond.

Although I'm sure I could have hit one of the Cows, I knew better. After watching me practice on hay bales, they rightfully concluded that I might be scheming to take a shot at them.

Cows: "Hey McNary kid. You're not planning on trying to shoot us with that are you?"

Me: "Um, well, it depends. You chase me through the pasture again and I just might."

Cows: "You do realize, you little idiot, that there are more of us than there are of you. You might get one of us, but we'll get you. And besides, we have a direct line to Jesus and if you try to take a shot at us, we'll tell him to rapture everyone else but leave you behind."

The Cows knew where to find my soft underbelly.

The tomahawk was a real flint-knapped stone that we found in a field. Plowed fields in Kansas sometimes reveal treasure troves of ancient Native American artifacts like flint arrowheads, hide scrapers, drills, knives and, yes, a tomahawk head. We found the head, fashioned a stick to make a handle like we'd seen in various drawings, and then covered it with blood from big, fat, gray ticks we'd pull off our dogs. We wanted it to look like we'd actually scalped a human being.

It was a communal tomahawk that Kendall and I shared and, yes, we lost it. Leave it up to a dumb little country kids to loose a thousand-year-old artifact. Oh, how I wish I had that back.

After much consideration, I finally chose the necessary items for the journey, rolled them up in a knapsack and tied it to my stick. I put on clean underwear, grabbed the bow, stuck the tomahawk in my belt loop, and bid my Mom farewell.

Me: "I'm leaving now. I'm running away from home."

Mom: "Did you get your bologna sandwich?"

Me: "Yes, thank you. Can I take one of your bottles of Pepsi, too?

Mom: "Nope."

Me: "Okay, well, I'll be leaving now. Tell Dad not to come looking for me when he gets   home."

Mom: "Okay. Call or write when you get wherever you're going."

I don't know if I was expecting her to wail, bargain with me, or throw a farewell party, but I was a bit put off with her apparent lack of interest.

Little boys have no sense about what time of the day it is. Unlike my forefathers who could look at the sun and tell you it was a-quarter-past-two, I only knew what time of the day it was by my Mom.

- It's time to get up.
- It's time to brush your teeth.
- It's time for lunch.
- It's time to come inside; it's going to be dark soon.
- It's time to put on clean underwear.

Once outside, I checked my compass and set a course for due east along Highway 54. It was late summer and the withered grass would make the trek easy.

I made it about two-hundred-yards and noticed something quite disconcerting; it was getting dark.

Mom: "Back so soon?"

Me: "Yeah, I forgot to pack extra underwear."

Mom: "They're in the dryer now; you'll have to wait 'till tomorrow."

Me: "Well, I really hate to, but I don't want to be in an accident without clean underwear."

Mom: "That's very wise of you. By the way, I made some extra chocolate pudding while you were gone. Want some?"

Me: "Oh, I suppose." Chocolate pudding was my kryptonite.

Mom: "Good, I'll get some whip cream for it too. There's always tomorrow to do what you started today."

A big bowl of chocolate pudding with whip cream and a good night's sleep gave me pause to reconsider my plans. Mom came into my room the next day as I was packing.

Mom: "Here's clean underwear for you."

Me: "Thanks, that's what I was waiting on. I can go now."

Mom: "That's probably best. I'm fixing liver-and-onions for dinner again tonight and I know you hate them."

Me: "Yes, yes, I do."

Mom: "But if you stay, I can fix you a hamburger."

Every man has a price for which his principles can be bought or sold. Mine was a hamburger.

I never attempted to run away from home again. And, to this day, I never leave home without wearing a clean pair of underwear.

Win Big At Rick's Shooting Gallery

When I was a kid, being bored was an entry-level crime in our house. *Idle hands are the devil's workshop,* Mom pontificated. She also kept a pitchfork in the broom closet for those times I either admitted to, or looked like, I was bored.

"Here," she'd hand me the pitchfork. "If you're bored, go clean out the horse barn."

"I'm not bored," I lied. "I'm meditating."

"Good. Go meditate with The Horse."

If you think cows are sarcastic, just walk up to a horse's barn with a pitchfork in your hand.

"Time for a little road-apple therapy, is it?" The Horse neighed. "Did our Mommy catch us being bored again? Love the

103

smell of horse-hockey on our boots, do we?"

I never did understand why The Horse talked to me in questions. Horses are the most beautiful animals on earth that can kill you with one well-aimed horseshoe. I'd sass back to a cow, but never a horse.

I don't remember being bored much except during the winter when it was so cold outside I'd wake up in the morning with The Horse in my bed. He put off enough body heat that I didn't mind, but horses are notorious for flatulence. He'd pass gas so loudly the covers on the bed rippled like a flag in the breeze.

But, again, a horse can kill you with one well-aimed horseshoe so I kept my mouth shut.

Country kids just don't get bored; there are too many things to explore, blow up, light on fire, tease until they chase you, or tempt fate with to ever want to stay inside and be bored. I see well-padded playgrounds today and think to myself, *we're raising sissies.* Atlantic Monthly has an article that agrees with me about why kids nowadays need to be exposed to the Things that Could Have Killed Me as a Kid.

We stayed outside from sun up to sun down because there were lots of adventures. That, and if we went inside, one of the adults quickly made indentured servants out of us. Running from the Cows of Hobson's Pond was much more fun than doing dishes.

Other than going a few miles down the road to church a few times a week, we seldom made the seven-mile journey to El Dorado, an oil town that carried the rotten-egg smell of crude oil on its boots.

However, we did make it to the County 4-H Fair once a year to check out the exhibits and ride as many rides as we could on the money we collected from 3-cents-a-pop- bottle returns.

I grew weary of the Ferris wheel and tried my luck with *The Bullet*, a torpedo-shaped apparatus that hung you upside down until all the change fell out of your pocket then loopty-looed you around in circles. Little kids learned to barf upside down riding *The Bullet*.

Still woozy from that ride, I stumbled over to the Shooting Galley. The straight-shooting gun must have been put there by mistake. Either that, or I was so cross-eyed from *The Bullet* that the crooked barrel of the gun aimed right where I couldn't focus. Anyway, in short order, I won a stuffed-animal the size of John Candy with a hair-do like Donald Trump. The carney finally told me, and the gun, he'd had enough of both of us and it was time for me to go barf on *The Bullet* again.

When I look back on my life to find the moment of inspiration to become an entrepreneur, it was that moment. I enjoyed the shooting gallery so much that I wanted to offer it to others, for a price of course, because that's what entrepreneurs do: find a way for people to pay for pleasure.

I returned to our five-acre spread in the country along Highway 54 and began The Official Strategic Business Plan for Rick's Shooting Gallery.

Since I wasted all of my capital at the County Fair, my low-budget plan left me without the option of building a new Shooting Gallery right along the well-traveled Highway. I surmised that since folks in the city would stop at a little kid's lemonade stand, then folks sizzling by at 70 miles-per-hour would hit the brakes if they saw my cherubic face imploring them to stop and try lady luck with my Daisy Red Ryder.

The next best option was the horse barn. However, first I had to negotiate with The Horse.

"I need you to move out of the barn for a while," I said.

"Why? You get kicked out of the house?" The Horse asked.

"No, I want to start a business. Can you see it now? In black spray paint on the corrugated-tin side of the barn: Rick's Shooting Gallery! Kind of like a neon sign only cheaper."

"Do I get a cut of the profits?" The Horse nickered.

After two hours of hard negotiation, we settled on an amicable arrangement that allowed him go into the barn at night and during thunderstorms, plus gave him a 40% cut on all profits. He was also required to let me paint "Rick's Shooting Gallery" in big, bold letters on his side; he was a walking billboard in the pasture.

Next, I had to make targets for customers to shoot. Dad had an old pair of tin-snips, rusted sheet metal, and baling wire so I cut out various shapes like stars and ducks. Then I hung them at varying depths and heights in the barn and put a two-by-four shelf in the door as a shooting rest to separate the customers from me, the proprietor.

I had only one granddaddy of a prize I could offer, a giant stuffed animal that looked like John Candy with a hair-do like Donald Trump. But I scrounged around for a while and came up with a slightly-used fishing pole, a metal bait bucket minus a handle, a seine net without poles and an antique tackle box we found buried in the creek bank. At least we called it antique. It's all about the story.

Next, I asked Kendall and Annie if they had any in-kind contributions to my new startup. Annie came back with an assortment of Barbie and Ken dolls needing surgery, matching apparel, and a Spirograph. Kendall returned with some slightly used cattle ear-tags and an empty paper-towel roll with matches scotch-taped to the end; he said it was a flashlight. At that time, that kind of flashlight had a national ethnicity to describe it, but I wouldn't dare call it that now less I offend almost everyone in America and half the population of Europe.

I wanted a huge billboard by the side of the road, but all my budget allowed was an old piece of plywood barely big enough to spray paint "Stop Now! Win Big! Rick's Shooting Gallery."

The only gun I had was a Daisy Red Ryder BB gun. I was forced with my first ethical business question: do I keep the barrel straight or bend it like the carneys were inclined to? I chose to be honest mainly because, if the business failed, I could still use the gun.

One of the hard lessons I learned as a ten-year-old entrepreneur was the importance of connecting product creation to product sales and marketing. You can have the best product in the world, but if you can't find a customer then you'll go bankrupt. My Shooting Gallery was a great product, but the problem was that my customers whizzed by at 70 miles-per-hour. My cherubic face and the appeal of winning big prizes was not enough for them to slam on the brakes.

Later, when I started my photography business, I asked the most respected and successful photographer what the key to success was and he said, "3 things: marketing, marketing, marketing. I know great photographers who can't sell postcards because they don't know how to market. I know mediocre photographers who have learned to market and are making a killing." As J.B. Clay and Floyd Hammer say, "Nothing happens until someone sells something."

The business went belly up after a few short days. My only customers were Kendall and Annie who wrote me I.O.U.s each time they played. However, they stopped after it dawned on them that they were winning back gifts they had donated.

In lieu of payment, The Horse made me clean his barn every day until the spray paint wore off his side. The cows, for once, expressed disappointment that my business scheme failed. They were much more supportive than I expected, but I later discovered The Horse told them that if I made a lot of money, they were all getting new barns. I may or may not have implied that in my negotiations with him.

Although I failed, at least I didn't go bankrupt. If I can ever get Kendall to pay me that three-dollar-and-fifty-cent I.O.U., then I can show a profit. But, he doesn't think he owes me since he gave me another paper-towel flashlight as a Christmas present that winter.

I tried various business opportunities listed on the backs of comic books such as selling greeting cards, raising sea monkeys, starting an ant farm, and x-ray glasses but soon discovered how the heavy-hand of government regulations crush small businesses. The Sheriff stopped by and told me to quit painting signs on the side of The Horse. Apparently, someone turned me in to the humane society.

I'm pretty sure it was the cows.

Whizzin' On the Christmas Presents

L ittle country boys enjoy the glorious freedom of taking a leak in the great outdoors anywhere and at anytime. He will not be inconvenienced during his escapades running home to Momma and the bathroom. Whizzin' outside is a little boy's divine right, his manifest destiny, and his heritage. Little boys seldom outgrow this love of nature. Some never do.

As we grew up in rural Kansas, we'd find the closest tree, or if no such obstructions were available, turn our backs to the group, unzip and let it rip. We even had contests. We've never outgrown that tendency either; we simply modified the methods, as we became adults. Just watch a group of executives in a board room and then imagine them being little boys out in a pasture. There's not much difference except they are in 3-piece suits instead of jean shorts.

However, the girls were not impressed. They shrieked, called us names, threatened to tattle, questioned our heritage then complained about life being unfair. Why weren't they given handy little spigots, too? In the battle of insults of which boys are inclined, the ultimate insult is to hurl this jab: "Oh, yeah, well you have to squat to whizz." Game over.

Furthermore, little boys are known to deliberately go outside to whizz instead of using the convenience of modern plumbing. They are not trying to save on water; they just feel *the call of nature.* Little boys seldom outgrow this tendency either. Some never do.

While this act of nature done in nature was, well, as natural for us as breathing, there is one notable story worth repeating.

Christmas arrived each year in time to keep us from turning all Jack-Nicholson-like in The Shining. Long winter nights without television in a drafty old two-story house are enough to turn Mother Teresa into Donald Trump. Since I was the last of six kids and the older siblings were gone, I was expected to entertain myself. It's hard to play Candyland by yourself.

I read every Hardy Boys book at least ten times and even snuck in a few Nancy Drew stories. Little boys just didn't read books about girls, but, since no one was around, I'd sneak Nancy in.

Old country houses have their own personality. Drive down a country road in your state and you will see what I mean. Some houses are like stately old patriarchs smoking a pipe with a glass of brandy. Others are like grizzled old cowboys with leathery skin from hours in the saddle, the sun and wind. Then there are houses that look like frumpy hypochondriac old ladies who would find something to gripe about if they won the lottery. Ours was that kind of house.

There is no sound as mournful as an old country house complaining about winter. When the temperature dipped below zero and the north wind howled across the prairie at 50 mph, our house complained more than a little old lady with bunions. So when Christmas started making its way down the road, we rejoiced as one rejoices over sedation for a root canal.

We celebrated with shepherds in bathrobes fawning over a plastic baby Jesus in the church play; a John Deere tractor pulled a hay wagon full of carolers down graveled roads; Dad made peanut brittle, popcorn balls and divinity – all things requiring root canals later in life. But the best part was being turned into pint-sized consumers salivating over the Sears Christmas catalog. Christmas was the best time of the year to feed our need for greed.

Kids today have no idea how big a deal the Sears Christmas catalog was to a bored little country kid. We didn't have the Internet and we weren't allowed to watch much television, so the only way to fill our greed was through Christmas catalogs. I literally flipped every one of the 969 pages of the catalog and chose an item from each page for my wish list. Twice. Maybe 3 times. The only exception was the women's clothing section; I ignored that until I was a teenager.

Allow me to digress; the 1975 Sears Catalog was quite a scandal. That year, on page 602, one of the male models appears to have his whizzer hanging low below the hem of his boxers. Scandalous, I say, scandalous! After numerous letters of protest, Sears said it was a blemish caused by a chemical falling on to the artwork during the printing process. So how many chemicals does it take to explain Miley Cyrus?

Furthermore, Mom couldn't let a good thing like Christmas go to waste without tossing in healthy dose of fear. We clearly understood that snooping for presents would result with burning coals in our stockings. Mom made such believers out of us we were afraid to open our own closets.

The only time I ever snooped was when I poked my head through a heat register in the upstairs floor and saw them wrapping a second-hand, football uniform for me. It was then I realized that we were poor. For some reason that second-hand Christmas gift was the best ever.

The Cows of Hobson's Pond

One happy Christmas, my sister Collen's kids were visiting and her baby boy did the dastardly deed inside the house, much to our delight.

Kelsey, otherwise known as Boo, was Toy's-R-Us adorable. Everyone loved sweet little Boo, especially my Dad – they were buds. On this glorious Christmas, Boo became our hero.

We had no clue what our presents were, regardless of how many times we shook them. Mine-is-bigger-than-yours seemed to matter for some dumb reason. Still does.

One evening, we were strewn about the living room on the naugahyde furniture watching The Charlie Brown Christmas Special with instructions to keep an eye on Boo. He was easy to watch, especially by the three of us who had a hard time keeping track of ourselves. One of us thought it would be funny to take Boo's diaper off and let him wander the house *a la naturale.*

No one paid much attention until he toddled over to the tree and took aim. Since it was a real tree, the smell of pine triggered his natural tendency to whizz, so he let it rip.

We were mortified until we realized that this little fireman hosing down the presents made the wrapping paper transparent. Slowly, like invisible ink starting to show, we began to identify our presents – we all got Spirographs. We giggled; Mom yelled at Boo; Boo began to cry; Dad came out of his study to rescue his little buddy. This was an-oft repeated cycle.

As exciting as it was to have the mysteries revealed, it slowly dawned on us that a cardinal rule had been violated: We saw our presents before Christmas. When that somber reality hit, all three of us looked at Mom much like a puppy being chided for pooping on the floor. We waited to have our noses rubbed in it.

Kendall, Boo's older brother, felt a need to argue on our behalf with this rationale:

- The three older kids were pure as the driven snow and had

112

not looked, no not even once, for our presents before Christmas. Did he mention we were pure as the driven snow?

- Boo was still young enough he couldn't form a coherent sentence so he was beyond the capacity to reason. Therefore, there was no premeditation.

- Therefore, we can only conclude it was an act of God.

Typically, Mom employed interrogation tactics that were the envy of the military. She authored *The Guantanamo Bay Interrogation Tactics* and was a senior advisor to the Gestapo and KGB.

However, we were fortunate that Mom witnessed the crime. Therefore, she avoided the typical interrogation methods of water boarding, stretching us out on the rack or staking us over an anthill.

As Kendall continued his opening statement, Mom held up her hands, walked back into the kitchen and muttered something about *who in their right mind took his diaper off and let a little kid walk around the house naked.* With her absence, we looked to the next authority figure to assess our fate.

Dad was still consoling Boo who was unaccustomed to being in trouble for anything. Ever. Although my Dad tried not to play favorites, Boo did have his own personal coat-of many-colors tailor.

"You guys better hurry and get that wrapping paper off of those presents or the dog will whizz on them, too," Dad said. "And, yes, you can play with your Spirographs."

Dad put a diaper back on Boo then we lifted him on our shoulders like faithful subjects carrying their king. He was our hero.

It occurs to me as I write this that the reason I've never seen history repeat itself is because we use fake Christmas trees. Fake pine trees do not prompt the natural tendencies in little boys to whizz on the presents. I've raised four boys and not one let loose on the tree.

But now I have a great idea! Excuse me, I need to run out and find a real tree: my grandsons are coming over for Christmas. I still think it would be funny to take a diaper off the littlest one and let him wander the house *a la naturale*.

It is, after all, his manifest destiny.

Epilogue

All of the stories in here are true, but I do confess to exaggerating the parts about the cows. In my own defense, making the cows like humans that could talk, reason, write and do basic math is normal. If you don't believe me, find a pet owner near you who treats their animal like family. I know people who have a complete conversation with their dogs or cats.

I also changed some names of the cows and people so I won't be sued. I'm certain that some cow alive today will read these stories and recognize that I was talking about her family. She'll call her to find the right cow attorney that sues people for ridiculous reasons and we'll end up in court. It happens more frequently than you know.

Writing Your Own Stories

I would give a lot of money to spend just one more day with my Dad. If I could, I'd set up video camera and have him tell me all the stories he told me when I was a kid.

Every writer has an audience in mind when put ink on paper or hammer out letters on a keyboard. My audience for this book is little people who can't read yet: my grandchildren.

Your stories matter.

If you want, I can help you tell your stories. Contact me through the information on the following page.

There is only one you and people want to hear your stories.

Other Books By Rick

Hunger Bites: Bite Size Stories of Inspiration

These are inspirational stories of people Rick has met along the way as he engages people in the fight against global hunger.

Voices on the Prairie

Sunny Morgan is left alone to run the Lonesome Star Ranch in the Flint Hills of Kansas. One morning, as she checks fence astride her horse, she watches a single engine airplane crash in front of her. She rescues Dane Richards, Governor of the State of Kansas and his brother-in-law.

The national attention Sunny receives thrusts her unwilling into the spotlight. However, she discovers hidden strengths as she confronts painful memories from her past and a new hope for the future.

All books are available to purchase on Amazon or from Whispering Meadows Company.

Contact: rick@whisperingmeadowscompany.com

Contact Information

Rick McNary
521 Whispering Meadows
Potwin, KS 67123

www.rickmcnary.me
rick@whisperingmeadowscompany.com

Phone: 316-734-6845

www.ingramcontent.com/pod-product-compliance
Lightning Source LLC
Chambersburg PA
CBHW060512030426
42337CB00015B/1861